C000054436

# Harold B. Barclay
# THE STATE

ANARCHIST POCKETBOOKS

# Harold B. Barclay

# THE STATE

**FREEDOM PRESS**
LONDON

Published in 2003 by
Freedom Press
84B Whitechapel High Street
London E1 7QX

© 2003 Freedom Press and Harold Barclay

ISBN 1 904491 00 6

Cover design by Clifford Harper and Jayne Clementson
Typeset by Jayne Clementson

Printed in Great Britain by Aldgate Press
Units 5/6 Gunthorpe Workshops, Gunthorpe Street, London E1 7RQ

# Contents

Introduction . . . . . . . . . . . . . . . . . . . . . . . . . . . . . . . . . . . . . . . . . 9

Chapter 1
What is a State? . . . . . . . . . . . . . . . . . . . . . . . . . . . . . . . . . . . . . 11

Chapter 2
The Variety of States . . . . . . . . . . . . . . . . . . . . . . . . . . . . . . . . . 27

Chapter 3
The Origin of the State . . . . . . . . . . . . . . . . . . . . . . . . . . . . . . . . 51

Chapter 4
The Modern State and its Future . . . . . . . . . . . . . . . . . . . . . . . 99

Bibliography . . . . . . . . . . . . . . . . . . . . . . . . . . . . . . . . . . . . . . . . 107

# INTRODUCTION

Much has been written about the nature of the state and the question of its origin and evolution. This essay is an addition to these works and hopefully a positive one. If it has any uniqueness it is in its dependence upon two main orientations. One is the empirical data of anthropology and archaeology, and the other is anarchist theory which may be seen as a specific expression of a more general conflict theory. I believe that the anthropological data sustain an anarchist theory of government. This theory, of course, rejects the state as fundamentally and inevitably despotic, and while it remains incontestable in terms of its critique of the state and any form of rule, it is less satisfactory in providing adequate mechanisms for achieving a truly free society. But, then, if it is not quite sufficient in this respect all the other alleged answers are far less credible.

A major segment of the population of the United States, and even more in Canada, believe that the state is a benign institution which aims to provide a variety of essential services. These include the provision of security against theft and injury, schools, libraries, good roads, sewerage, disaster relief, defence of the homeland, fair weights and measures, protection of food quality and other goods. No doubt the list could be considerably extended. Without the state it is claimed we would have none of these.

This point of view is totally at odds with the anarchist view and in the course of this essay I intend to address the issues raised then by these conflicting notions. We may inquire how is it that the great mass of people so eagerly and willingly submit to the state, especially when history shows that the state is an oppressive and abusive institution of rather recent appearance and that for thousands of years humans lived on this earth quite successfully without the state? If the state is oppressive why does it provide so many social services? Or how did the idea of the state originate anyway? Is there any alternative to state organisation?

A major part of this essay will concern the several factors which might be necessary requirements for state formation. Of major importance here is the development of hierarchy – of differences in access to power and wealth.

I have tried throughout to avoid the use of jargon and neologisms, although this cannot be totally successful since in any field of endeavour it becomes necessary to introduce certain technical terms.

# Chapter I
# What is a State?

Our first task in this undertaking is to clarify what we are talking about. There are several terms used in popular discourse which are relevant to this discussion and deserve some specification. These are society, law, power, authority, state and government. In addition, I introduce social sanctions, which should aid in further understanding how human societies work.

## Society

It is one of the universal myths in our modern world, a myth propagated by the state, that particularly seeks to confuse the idea of the state with society. Indeed, the two are often equated, if only to further the belief that life is not possible without the state. Elsewhere, I have attempted to show that society and life in general are perfectly possible without the state; we do not require the state to provide 'law and order' (See *People without Government: an anthropology of anarchy*).

Society is a term which may apply to the social life of innumerable other animals besides humans. A society is any group of organisms which interact socially with one another over a prolonged period and, in so doing, evince a degree of mutual dependence and reciprocity, and distinguish themselves from other similar collectivities with which they do not have such intense interaction and dependence.

A society by definition has order and structure and operates with regularised, relatively fixed modes of behaviour. The term society implies that the component members are operating according to some 'rules of the game'. For other animals these rules are mostly genetic in origin or, to use a perhaps old fashioned term, they are instinctive, whereas for humans they are primarily acquired through learning and are part of a cultural tradition.

Rules may be quite vague and open to conflicting interpretations or they may be very specific and explicit. In any case there are guidelines without which we would be lost in sea of *anomie*. Part of the problem in the modern world is that many of these guidelines have become so ambiguous that the level of general anxiety increases. It is clear that where there is no structure, there is no order and there is no society. And, as the first lesson in any anthropology or sociology course points out, humans without society are not human. But another part of that first lesson is that there is an enormous amount of variation within human society, including the amount and kind of structure and order.

Having said this, let me add that humankind often seeks a holiday from routine and structure. Max Gluckman pointed to what he called 'rituals of rebellion', which are periods in which the populace is expected to behave – within limits – in a manner counter to normal expectation. Thus there is the 'Mardi Gras', which is a traditional relaxing of behaviour before the commencement of the exacting observations of the Lenten season. We have Halloween as a traditional time when children are permitted a short expression of rebellion against the adult world.

Victor Turner has suggested that there are two countercurrents in a society: one of structure and the other of *communitas* or anti-structure. The latter expresses the spontaneous, the unplanned and the ecstatic, as a kind of reaction to the usual, predictable and structured. This is in a way similar to Proudhon's view that authority and liberty operate as antinomies within any society, each acting so as to delimit the other.

But Proudhon also said that liberty is the mother of order not the daughter. The individual or group which has sufficient liberty to be self-regulating will have the highest degree of order; the imposition of order from above and outside induces resentment and rebellion, where it does not encourage childlike dependence and impotence, and so becomes a force for disorder – all points which have considerable bearing on the ensuing discussion of the nature of the state.

Most human societies which have existed had no government, no law and no state. Prior to about 4000BCE none of these entities existed. As we shall see, the state actually has a 'pristine' origin, a purely independent invention, in only a very few places in the world. The great mass of human cultures adopted the idea from one or the other of at most a half dozen 'pristine' forms and for most of them it was imposed by force.

## Social Sanctions

In stateless or anarchic societies order exists as in other human societies because people live according to the rules. How people behave is monitored by one's fellows. Radcliffe-Brown* proposed the term 'sanctions' to apply to the manner in which a social group reacts to the behaviour of any one of its members. Thus a positive sanction is some form of expression of general approval. A soldier is given a medal, a scholar an honourary degree, or a student an award. Mother kisses little junior for his good behaviour, or daddy gives him a piece of candy. A negative sanction is the reaction of the community against the behaviour of a member or members; it expresses disapproval. The soldier may be court martialed, the scholar fired or put in jail. The student may be given a failing grade in a course or ostracised by his fellows, and the child may be slapped by his parent. Of course, negative sanctions become the most important in any society.

Sanctions may also be categorised as being 'diffuse', 'religious' or 'legal'. Here my interpretation deviates slightly from that of Radcliffe-Brown. Diffuse sanctions are those which are

---

* According to Alan Barnard, A.R. Radcliffe-Brown was known to his friends in university as Anarchy Brown because of his political sympathies (70).

spontaneously applied by any one or more members of the community. Crucial to the conception of diffuse sanctions is the notion that their application is not confined to the holder of a specific social role. They may be imposed by anyone within a given age/sex grade or, occasionally, there may be no limit to who may initiate them. This is the meaning of diffuse: responsibility for and the right to impose the sanction is spread out over the community. Society as a whole has the power. There is no special elite which even claims a monopoly on the use of violence as a sanctioning device. Further, when and if sanctions are applied is variable, as is the intensity of the sanctions imposed.

Diffuse sanctions include gossip, name-calling, arguing, fist-fighting, killing and ostracism. Duelling and formal wrestling matches are less widespread forms. Inuit have ritualised song competitions in which two opponents try to outdo one another before an audience which acts as judge. Diffuse sanctions may be resorted to by an individual or a group. And their effectiveness is enhanced as the entire community joins in its expression of disapproval. Vigilante style action and feuds are common forms of diffuse sanctions which depend upon collective action. While many of these sanctions are violent, it should be borne in mind that invariably with even the hint of violence mediation mechanisms are launched to settle issues.

In many societies fines and other punishments are meted out by an assembly. Radcliffe-Brown calls these 'organised' sanctions. They are still not 'legal', but have the character of diffuse sanctions of a more formalised type *if* the assembly lacks the authority to use force in executing its decision, which is a very common feature in such arrangements. In such instances, the assembly acts as a mediator rather than as judge or arbitrator and is successful to the extent that it can convince two disputing parties to come to some compromise.

Diffuse sanctions are a universal form of social regulation; if a social group has nothing else it will have various techniques which can readily be classified as diffuse sanctions.

Religious sanctions involve the supernatural. 'Black magic' may be performed against a person; one may be threatened with the eternal torments of hell, or encouraged with positive sanctions promising everlasting ecstasy in heaven. The Nuer leopard skin chief may get his will done by threatening to curse another person. The Ojibwa Indians believed infractions of the rules led to the acquisition by supernatural means of specific kinds of disease. Thus, religious sanctions may either have a human executor, as in the case of a curse, or be seen as automatic, as with the Ojibwa belief, or the idea that breaking one of the ten commandments commits one to hell. In another respect, religious sanctions are either those which are intended to bring forth punishment in this world, or those which are for an after-life: physical versus ultimate spiritual punishment. Positive religious sanctions will also provide rewards in this world and in the after life. Religious sanctions can produce priesthoods whose powers parallel those of secular police and judges.

Legal sanctions involve all expressions of disapproval or approval of the behaviour of an individual wherein:

a) such expressions are specifically delegated to persons holding defined roles, one of the duties of which is the execution of these sanctions;

b) these individuals alone have the 'authority' to threaten use of violence and to use it in order to carry out their job, and;

c) punishments meted out in relation to the infraction are defined within certain limits and in relation to the 'crime'.

Policemen, justices of a court, jailers, executioners and lawmakers are examples of those who may enforce legal sanctions. In our society they collectively constitute the government. The state through its agent the government declares its monopoly on the use of violence against others within society, meaning that only certain agents of the state, for example policemen, can take a person off the streets and put him in jail. Only certain collectivities, that is courts, can determine guilt or innocence and assess appropriate punishments that are in accord with what others, namely lawmakers, have established as law.

Legal sanctions are laws. Laws exist where one has specific social roles designed to enforce regulations, by force of violence if necessary, and where punishment has certain defined limits. Laws exist where you have government and the state; conversely, if you have government you have law. Legal sanctions, and thus law and government, are not universal, but are characteristic of only some human societies – albeit the most complex ones. Such societies also, it should be borne in mind, retain a peripheral position for both diffuse and religious sanctions.

Malinowski suggested that the term 'law' should be applied loosely to cover all social rules which have the support of society. Such usage, however, obscures the fundamental and important difference in the means by which different rules are enforced. Law and government are invariably associated with rule by an elite class, while governmentless societies are invariably egalitarian and classless. Hence, Malinowski's loose usage obfuscates the important difference concerning who, or what, enforces regulations.

## Power and authority

The relation between power and authority is another often misunderstood area. In human groups some manoeuvring for power characterises the relationship between individual members. The intensity and emphasis on the contest varies from one culture to another and from one individual to another. The cultural values of the Pygmies and also of such Pueblo Indians as the Zuni and Hopi play down attempts by individuals to stand in the forefront, although one cannot say that the desire to influence others is absent. And within every culture we find that some people strive more than others and a few even opt out. Nevertheless, the contest for power manifests itself in some fashion within each human group.

Power means the ability to get others to do what you want them to do. Someone who convinces ten others to follow orders has more power than someone who is able to get only one to obey. This depends on all other things being equal, since, for example, someone who controls the one individual who knows how to use a nuclear detonating device can have more power than someone who controls a million ordinary men and women. There is also a collective kind of power, according to Parsons, in which individuals cooperate to bring their joint power to bear on a third party (199 *ff.*).

Power means influence – convincing others by logical argument, by the prestige of one's status or rank, by money or bribe. Or it means implied or overt threat of injury – either psychological or physical – and the ability to carry it out.

The contest for power is an important dynamic force in society and it is a major mechanism by which a society changes over time.

The 'push and pull' of members not only causes 'palace revolutions', that is, shifts in the personnel of the less powerful and the more powerful, but leads as well to changes in rules and values.

Ralf Dahrendorf, a German sociologist, suggested that the conflict for power is central in a society. Marx was primarily concerned with one feature of the power complex, namely economic power. This emphasis has meant that those who follow Marx devalue the non-economic dimensions of power. Consequently we find peoples' democracies in which the oppression of ordinary people is no less than it was before the 'revolution'. Marxism in practice has tended to transfer the forces of power from the capitalist to the professional bureaucrat and military officer, primarily because it does not see that the central problem is the problem of power itself.

Max Weber stressed the difference between power and authority. In any society individual members recognise certain others as having authority within specific realms. Thus, in modern society members accept as *legitimate* the right of certain individuals to carry and, where necessary, to employ firearms, in order to apprehend suspected law breakers. These policemen invariably wear special dress. Members of this society do not recognise as legitimate the use of force by others, such as gangsters. In both cases coercive force is employed. In the first the power is authority since it is accepted as legitimate and right; but the second is not authority; it is the illegitimate use of power. Something of this kind of distinction can be identified in all societies. Yet a significant modification of Weber's terminology is necessary. Most Canadians would eagerly subscribe to the notion that the power of the Ottawa government is legitimate, but some would only acquiesce to that power. The several generations of colonial rule by the Dutch in Indonesia, for example, commenced as a pure case of the imposition of brute force. But with the passage of time it acquired a certain 'legitimation', so that the power became authority in Weber's sense. But it becomes legitimate power because the Indonesians learned to acquiesce; they grew accustomed to the situation and tacitly accepted it. Raymond Firth has noted that power acquires some kind of support from the governed either because of "routine apathy, inability to conceive of an alternative or acceptance of certain values regarded as unconditional" (123). Most authority commences as the raw power of the gangster and evolves into a respectable legitimate authority of tacit acquiescence. This certainly is the history of the nation-state. Fried observed that legitimacy is the means by which ideology is blended with power. The function of legitimacy is "to explain and justify the existence of concentrated social power wielded by a portion of the community and to offer similar support to specific social orders, that is, specific ways of apportioning and directing the flow of social power" (26).

No one accepts the legitimacy of 'raw' use of power, nor does anyone reject completely any and all kinds of authority. Even the anarchist recognises that there is a place for legitimate authority. Proudhon once remarked, "… if man is born a sociable being, the authority of his father over him ceases on the day when his mind being formed and his education finished, he becomes the associate of his father …" (264). Later Bakunin wrote: "We recognise, then, the absolute authority of science … Outside of this only legitimate authority, legitimate because it is rational and is in harmony with human liberty, we declare all other authorities false, arbitrary and fatal" (Maximoff, 254).

Paul Goodman in *Drawing the Line* writes of natural coercion in which the infant is dependent upon his mother or the student upon the teacher – cases in which teaching is involved with the intent of increasing the independence of the one to attain the level of the other (1946). Fromm also distinguishes between 'rational' and 'irrational' authority. Rational authority has its source in competence; it requires constant scrutiny and criticism and is always temporary. It is based upon the equality of the authority and the subject "which differ only with respect to the degree of knowledge or skill in a particular field … The source of irrational authority, on the other hand, is always power over people – either physical or mental power" (9).

Stanley Milgram has said that people appear to believe that those in positions of authority, including politicians, are the most knowledgeable. But perhaps this is only wishful thinking in an attempt to justify their authorities. People delude themselves into thinking that through the electoral process they put the intellectually superior into office.

Modern society has many in authority who have earned rationally the right to authority, but it has many whose claim to authority is irrational and they are our politicians, judges and policemen. There are specialists, that is authorities in various realms, who are accepted as such because of their expertise. Yet one can readily see the potential danger inherent even here, that those holding one form of authority may seek to extend their power so that rational authority is transformed into irrational authority. Most of us will at least have heard of the physician who assumes a position as 'world's foremost authority' on everything.

Closely related to the concept of authority is that of leadership. Although group leadership is a universal of human social organisation, it is, at the same time necessary to stress that leadership is conceived differently amongst different peoples. The Pygmies and Hopi of Arizona express a distrust of leaders, such that each individual seeks to avoid the leadership role, blending into the group as much as possible.

Since societies have order and structure and must deal with the problem of power, they are therefore involved in politics. Not only do all societies have politics, but they have political organisation – that is, standardised ways of dealing with power problems. Political organisation is not a synonym for government. Government is *one* form of political organisation. Politics may be handled in a variety of ways; government is just one of those ways. Anarchists might suggest the application of certain forms of diffuse sanctions.

In the broadest sense politics can be applied to any kind of social group. That is, there may even be politics within the family – where clearly the distribution of power between father, mother and children is a major issue. A local club also has politics in a similar small-scale fashion. Ordinarily, however, when one speaks of politics or political organisation, one does not think of the internal affairs of the family. Political organisation applies more to 'public' affairs – relations which are territorial and cut across kinship groupings. Politics involves a substantial geographical area – a community, or at least an extensive neighbourhood, as well as an entire nation-state. Yet even this kind of conceptualisation leads to ambiguity as to whether one is dealing with political or family affairs. We may have a confrontation between two groups related by kinship, but beyond the level of an extended family (for example, two patrilineages), which would be considered at least as a quasi-public affair. Nevertheless, the terms of address employed and the atmosphere of the exchange will unmistakably be those of kinship.

## Government and the state

Conceptions of government and the state and the relationship between them are often confused. I have already intimated above something of the nature of these two entities, but here will address the meaning of these terms directly.

Nadel has given three specific characteristics of the state and in so doing has also indicated the role of government in the state (69-70). First, the state is a territorial association. It claims 'sovereignty' over a given place in space and all those residing within that area are subject to, and must submit to the institution of authority ruling that territory, that is, the government. In several earlier states boundaries between them were sometimes vague and not defined. For instance this was true of the several West African states which existed several centuries ago. In such cases authority was most clear in the vicinity of the capital city and tended to become less definite as one reached to peripheries. Even today there is no fixed boundary between most of Yemen and Saudi Arabia, but this remains an exception to the rule.

While the state is a territorial entity, it is often an inter-tribal and inter-racial structure. The criteria for membership are determined by residence and birth. Membership is ordinarily ascribed, although one may voluntarily apply to join if one immigrates and seeks to settle within the territory of the state.

The state has an apparatus of government and this is to some degree centralised. The government functions to execute existing laws, legislate new ones, maintain 'order', and arbitrate conflicts to the exclusion of other groups or individuals. It comprises specific individuals holding defined social roles or offices. Crucial to the definition of such roles is the claim to a monopoly of the legitimate use of violence within the territory. The part played by the different role holders in using violence may vary so that there can be a highly differentiated system of division of labour (*cf.* discussion of legal sanctions above). All are in any case part of a single integrated monopolistic institution. Such a situation differs, for example, from the role of the Inuit shaman who may threaten a victim with violence, since the shaman cannot claim any monopoly on its legitimate use. In some states the central Government may be so weak it cannot lay any monopolistic claim to using force. There may be powerful competing elements within the territory, so laying the basis for civil war. Or a weak state may find its sovereignty compromised by a dominating and powerful neighbour as is the case with modern Lebanon with Syria on the one hand and Israel on the other. The sovereignty of Latin American states may also be questioned in the face of the influence of the United States. Yet all states at least profess the myth that they are sovereign and possess ultimate authority.

The ruling group in any state tends to be a specialised and privileged body separated by its formation, status and organisation from the population as a whole. The group collectively monopolises political decision. In some polities it may constitute an entrenched and self-perpetuating class. In other more open systems such as a democracy, there is a greater circulation or regular turnover of membership of the ruling group, so that dynasties or other kinds of closed classes of rulers do not ordinarily occur. This, of course, contributes to the illusion of equality of power in a democracy and obscures the division between rulers and ruled.

Fundamental to both government and the state is the employment of violence to enforce the law. This may be variously viewed as either imposition of the will of the ruling group, or as a device to maintain order, keep the peace and arbitrate internal conflicts. In fact states and governments fulfil all these functions by enforcing the law. Others have emphasised that the paramount and ultimate end of all law enforcement is to benefit the ruling interests, even though there may be positive side effects such as keeping the peace. They would further emphasise that the existence of the state is conducive to strife and conflict since, as a system based upon the use of violence, it thereby legitimises and incites it. The state is further predicated upon the assumption that some should be bosses giving orders while others should be subordinates – a situation which can only irk the subordinates and frustrate them and, thus, become yet another provocation of violence. Democratic systems may ameliorate this condition, but they do not cure it. By their nature state and government discourage, if they do not outlaw, the natural voluntary cooperation among people. Thomas Hobbes held that without government, society is nasty and brutish, but we could as well turn old Hobbes on his head and say that the world might be more peaceful and people more able to assume personal responsibility and cooperate with others if there were no state. And, clearly, the anthropological record does not support Hobbes. Stateless societies seem less violent and brutish than those with the state.

The state is an organisation for war and no more efficient mechanism for war has been developed. War was invented by the state. It took a powerful complex structure like a state to organise armies. I propose to consider the relationship between war and the state more fully in Chapter 3, under 'Military Organisation'.

It is well to recognise that it seems impossible to divest ourselves of all forms of coercion, even in a stateless condition. Such diffuse sanctions as ostracism and gossip can be as fully oppressive as the law of the state. Nevertheless with the state there is always a hierarchical and status difference between rulers and ruled. Even if it is a democracy, where we suppose that those who rule today are not rulers tomorrow, there are still differences in status. In a democratic system, only a tiny minority will ever have the opportunity to rule and these are invariably drawn from the elite. Differential status is not inherent in diffuse sanctions. Where a group or individual employs gossip or ostracism against another person, that person may freely use these same techniques. Where we have the command position of a father over his son, however, we do have a form of coercion which approaches that of government. Yet still the father role has the quality of a rational authority and a young man may expect eventually to 'graduate' to a position of greater equality with his father, eventually achieving fatherhood himself. In no diffuse sanction is there a vesting of power into the hands of a restricted group of commanders. Further, one would assume that in a more enlightened stateless society social sanctions would stress conflict resolution, mediation and conciliation rather than punishment.

From one point of view nothing is purely voluntary and all acts are seen as being in some way coerced. Conscience, ego, 'id', 'the inner spirit' or what have you, are fully as coercive forces as the policeman or public ostracism. However, coercion may be better conceived as a relationship of command and obedience, wherein the commanding force is always external to the individual person. Such a force can be other humans or the supernatural. From this point of view the commands of my conscience are not coercion, at least not of the same order.

## Conclusion

The classification of sanctions discussed above may now be summarised in relation to political systems by means of the following diagram, presented as a continuum with anarchy, where there is no government, at one end and archy, where the state and government clearly exist, at the other. Under anarchy only diffuse and those supernatural sanctions which derive directly from non-human sources are operative. There is an emphasis upon voluntary cooperation and disputes are settled by mediation. In archy there is the prevalence of legal sanctions and the rule by arbitration. Between the two poles, there is a limbo which may be seen as marginal forms of anarchy or as rudimentary governments. There are anomalous cases of this kind and we shall consider one of these later. Such entities may possibly represent transitional examples from anarchy to state. As Lowie has said, states do not appear full blown out of the stateless condition; they too must evolve or develop and this takes time.

Anarchy                                    Archy

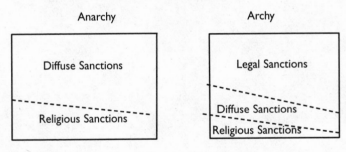

This continuum should not be interpreted as an evolutionary scheme in which cultural history is a one way street where all 'tribal' societies must become state type societies. It does appear, however, that the main thrust of history is the transformation of stateless societies into state ones. Why this should be is another question to be addressed in the remainder of this essay. In any case, let us not forget that even if the trend of history favours the change from anarchy to archy, this does not thereby make that process right and good.

# Chapter 2

# The Variety of States

The state cannot be viewed as a monolithic entity that is eternally the same from its inception to the present, from America to Asia. States vary especially in their degree of despotism, in the extent of their bureaucracy, and their overall organisation. As there are many kinds of states, there are several ways of classifying them.

First, however, let us dispose of the problem of the anomalous, the ambiguous or marginal state. The Anuak of the southern Sudan perhaps institute the office of 'king', with its symbolic trappings, but stripped of its powers. These horticultural people live in villages each of which has a headman who holds 'court' and keeps sacred emblems of the village such as drums and beads. He is approached by others with signs of respect such as obeisance and the use of a special vocabulary. Although his house is no better than anyone else's, the fence posts are decorated with the skulls of animals killed to provide feasts he offers his people. While he has the superficial symbols of kingship, the headman has little power and is largely at the mercy of his fellow villagers. As long as he can provide feasts he has good standing and his villagers will see to it that he is shown proper respect. He is, with the help of third parties, able to persuade, for example, both the killer of a fellow villager to make compensation and the victim's kin to accept it.

Anuak do not believe a man should hold the headship for very long and, definitely, one who cannot properly feast his followers deserves no support. He will then find his followers deserting him. A major faction opposing the headman will arise and install a rival who must be the son of some previous headman. Such an event leads to fighting in which the old headman may be deposed.

Despite the quarrelling and intrigue which surrounds the headman office, it does operate as a unifying force in village affairs, which are otherwise defined by a segmentary lineage – that is, a kinship arrangement. Although different factions appear in a village, they are not revolutionary: no one seeks to abolish the position of headman.

In south-eastern Anuakland, headmen are drawn only from a 'noble' clan which apparently comes from outside the Anuak country. Necklaces, spears, stools and drums are emblems of the office and there is much struggle, intrigue and fighting to obtain possession of them. The holder has, as elsewhere among the Anuak, little authority in his own village, but he can mobilise an armed force on occasion and sometimes extend his influence and gain a tenuous control over neighbouring villages.

Thus, among the Anuak, we see the beginnings of a centralisation of authority, based upon a ceremonial and symbolic role and the ability to be the centre of a redistribution – feasting – process. And in the south-east of the area the 'kingly' role becomes recognisably predatory. But in such an arrangement there appears to be only the most minimal application of legal sanctions, the signs of a true state. Perhaps the Anuak might be considered a proto-state displaying a greater potentiality for state development than more legitimately stateless societies (*cf.* Chapter 3).

For the remainder of this chapter I propose to briefly consider true states and their varying kinds. First, there is the difference between the pristine state and the secondary. Following this the size of states will be considered and lastly the type of polity or form of government.

## Pristine and secondary states

States have been referred to as pristine or secondary in which the former is a purely autochthonous creation, invented independently of any other influence. The secondary state is derived or imposed from another; it is not original. There is some controversy over how many pristine states there are. In any case, the point is that there are very few. The state was not an idea that readily came to mind. However, a society may teach a degree of hierarchy and property differences that drive it into statehood. The fourth millenium BCE is the period of initial state formation in both Mesopotamia and Egypt. Other pristine states may include India, China and the Olmec of Mexico, along with the Polynesian island groups of Hawaii, Tahiti, Tonga and Samoa. Most questionable in this category is India because the state appeared shortly after those in Mesopotamia and it is extremely close to Mesopotamia geographically, suggesting the good possibility of diffusion rather than independent invention. Due primarily to the extreme isolation of the Olmec and Polynesians from any states elsewhere, it is most likely that they were pristine.

Of the secondary states I would argue that the vast majority of them have had the state thrust upon them by external forces rather than adopting the idea voluntarily. Today every inch of earth along with thousands of square miles of open sea are claimed by one state or another. Compare this to 1492 when all of Australasia, most of Siberia, Sub-Saharan Africa, North and South America had no states. Presently there are 192 presumably independent states covering this planet, but of these 158 have arisen out of a colonial situation. All of the 35 states of North and South America were parts of the British, French, Spanish, Portuguese or Dutch empires and 50 of the 52 African states were likewise carved out of European colonial empires. The fourteen states of Oceania were manufactured from previous British and French and American colonies. Even in Europe 24 of its 44 states were once parts of the British, Russian, Austro-Hungarian, Ottoman or Danish empires. And in Asia 35 of its 47 states were until recent times parts of one empire or another.

The state structure and governments of all these 158 states were modelled on already existent forms, usually in some considerable detail. Most commonly, former British colonies took on the trappings of British governance while former French colonies copied the French. Most of the former Spanish colonies were heavily influenced by the American and French revolutions. In any case one would be hard put to find any which did not closely follow a European pattern.

It should, however, be pointed out that perhaps 40 of these 158 states once claimed status as sovereign nations prior to being colonised, and that in about a dozen African states there once existed states which claimed at least part of their present respective countries. Nevertheless, this does not distract from the fact that the great majority of existent states are such because the state was imposed upon the inhabitants by force.

States have also arisen out of response to being in close proximity to existing large states. The several Germanic peoples lived for generations along the borders of the Roman Empire and numerous so-called tribes, chiefly pastoralists, inhabited the edges of the Chinese and Iranian empires. Particularly in the latter case, notables acted as intermediaries with the giant states and were central figures in the very important trade between China and the West. Through such channels these notables were able to enhance their wealth and power and became recognised by their powerful neighbours as rulers and heads of states in their own right. In part at least, one might say these states were created out of necessity, the necessity of dealing and trading with great empires.

Among Afghan tribes, men of influence have assumed the role of chief liaison agent between their own people and the neighbouring state. Increasingly they come to accumulate the trappings of governmental authority themselves and so create states. Similarly, European colonial powers in the process of their territorial aggrandisement, on contact with people in stateless societies, recognised certain individuals as 'chiefs of the tribe' and insured for them formalised power positions. A widespread feature of both American and Canadian relations with their aboriginal populations has been the imposition of a system of tribal chiefs and tribal or band councils with limited police powers where in pre-contact times there was no such authority. The instillation of this statist orientation has even led to many Indian groups calling themselves sovereign nations. It has been argued that in West Africa, raiding parties, in harassing their acephalous neighbours, led the latter to introduce centralised political power as a defence mechanism. Thus, existing states breed a statist mentality where it did not exist before.

The Medieval Arab historian, Ibn Khaldun, drawing on Middle Eastern history, argued for an ongoing dialectic between the nomadic pastoral tribe and the urban-oriented state. The former was a stateless community based upon a sense of social solidarity. In the course of events it invaded and conquered a decaying urban state and for a time reinvigorated it with the new rule of tribal chiefs become rulers of state. Eventually this situation leads to decay and corruption and exposes the state to invasion and domination by a new wave of nomads inspired by the wealth and glitter of the city. This process is presumably repeated over and over, in each case the stateless society of nomads embraces a state organisation.

In sum, then, the overwhelming majority of states are not original inventions, but have been inspired by external influences and in most cases the major external influence has been the force of violence. Yet at the same time these copycat states bore in their background most or all of the preparatory characteristics, which will be discussed in the next chapter, that caused the original pristine states to appear.

## The size of states

States may also be classified according to relative size, where size includes a consideration of populations, area, military strength and wealth. We may speak of maximal, major, modest and minor states. Today there is only one maximal state, the United States of America, whereas in 1940, aside from the United States, there was the USSR, the United Kingdom, Germany and, perhaps, France. Major states would now include the three foregoing nations, Russia, Japan, China and, most probably, India. The modest states would include Italy, Brazil, Mexico, Canada and Indonesia among others. Minor states might include countries such as Sweden, Spain, Egypt, Iraq, Vietnam and South Africa, while any state with less than a million population would belong in the category of micro-states, which number a total of 41 (varying from the Vatican to Swaziland).

This classification exposes the immense difference between states, especially in relation to their power. On the whole one can discount the micro-states while minor states operate as important actors in their immediate neighbourhoods, being unable to compete on an international stage. (They can, however, act as minor irritants on this stage, as is the case of Iraq *vis à vis* the United States and Great Britain).

States change their positions on the world stage from time to time. Few would recall that Sweden was once a major power in the Europe of the seventeenth and eighteenth centuries. And five hundred years ago England was a very minor player in the state game, but rose to pre-eminence in the eighteenth and nineteenth centuries to a maximal position in the early twentieth, only to decline sharply after World War Two. The United States arose out of nothingness to become *the* single great power in the world.

As all states change, they also have a life span. Few seem to pass the thousand year mark, although pre-Hyksos Egypt, Babylon and ancient China lasted much longer. There are even those which live for a short while and disappear only to be resurrected again (e.g. Poland, Lithuania). If our past history tells us anything it is that any state will eventually pass into oblivion – even the United States of America. This, then, raises yet another question: why should states decline and disappear? Let us briefly consider this issue.

## The decline of states

Why states inevitably decline and die has been the subject of innumerable lengthy tomes authored by well known philosophers of history from Gibbon to Spengler and Toynbee, as well as anthropologists and sociologists.* It is pretentious of me to attempt to address such a topic, especially in this short essay. But perhaps to provide some completeness to the subject of the state I might present a brief laundry list of some of the issues involved, derived from various sources.

In some respects the decline of a state is a mirror image of its rise. Obviously some factors are of more central importance in the process while others more contributory. That is, some important condition or conditions may impel the state onto its downward slope, as others can further push it to destruction.

One central factor is that a state may be unable to adapt to changing circumstances. An ascending state makes tremendous investments in the technology and organisation of the time. New technologies and more efficient forms of organisation later arise with which new states, unburdened by the old, can take advantage. The older state remains chained to what are becoming antiquated ways because it has made such an investment in them and its position as an important power lends itself to conservatism. The rise of Japan as a major competitor to the United States and Great Britain is a case in point. One might also ponder what would happen if some state successfully developed a cheap and renewable energy source while all the others remained dependent on fossil fuels. In a more abstract vein, A.L. Kroeber

---

* See Tainter (pages 39-90) for a review and assessment of various attempts to explain the 'collapse' of complex society.

spoke of pattern exhaustion, by which he meant that a civilisation may accept one pattern in the arts or philosophy and explore it so thoroughly as to exhaust all its possible ramifications.

A state may over-extend itself, becoming so large as to become unmanageable with its established methods of administration and its available resources. Again this involves in part an inability to adapt. Further, the larger a state becomes the greater is the possibility that those distant from the centres of power – those at the frontiers – can break off and form separate and opposing states. Over-extension was no doubt important in the decline of the Roman, Ottoman and Alexandrian Greek empires.

Perhaps Great Britain is an example of a state which went into decline as a result of exhaustion from warfare, in the British case, two horrendous wars within twenty years. But at the same time Germany is an example of a state which went through the same two wars and at greater expense, at least to recover as the most prosperous European economy, albeit not the military power it was in 1940. Further, of course, states may be totally defeated in warfare and absorbed by the victor.

The nature of the state administration is worthy of note. Highly centralised and large bureaucratic organisations eventually work against the success of the state. Certainly this was important to the downfall of the Soviet system, which was so highly centralised that a factory worker in the provinces could hardly obtain a monkey-wrench unless he had permission in the form of much red tape from Moscow. Yet even less centralised structures can be excessively burdensome if they are poorly organised and inefficient or infested with corruption. Competing elites within the ruling class may engage in a self-destructive struggle.

Those who have advocated a great man theory of history emphasise that the greatness of a state is dependent upon having great leaders. The greatness of the state here refers to its significance as a world power and major influence in international affairs. Great leaders may be charismatic personalities or they may be astute, shrewd and ruthless manipulators after Machiavelli's Prince or they may, and more probably are, both of these at the same time. Presumably, then, if a state is headed by poor, incompetent and non-charismatic leaders it should decline.

I find any correlation between a charismatic 'prince' and a powerful state to be problematical. The charismatic Winston Churchill could not rescue Britain from its inevitable decline. The charismatic Hitler, Mussolini and Napoleon led their states to destruction. The United States has had a series of charismatic manipulators (Jefferson, Jackson, Lincoln, T. Roosevelt and F.D. Roosevelt) interspersed between long lists of the undistinguished. There is little correlation with the mounting importance of the United States. Many great leaders seem to be like wisps in the night (Alexander, Kublai Khan, Attila). They appear and are followed by nonentities. More important than any individual to the rise or decline of the state may be the character and nature of its ruling elite.

One cause of decline is appropriate for modern times and that is massive pollution of essential resources – water, soil and air. In the past this has not been as common. In ancient Iraq continual irrigation eventually caused salinisation which threatened the welfare of the state. Today fossil fuels, herbicides, and pesticides coupled with questionable agricultural and forestry practices have the makings for potential disaster.

Once a state has peaked and commences a decline, that decline may be expedited further by a variety of natural disasters: volcanic eruptions, earthquakes, floods, fires, famines and epidemics. However, famines and epidemics may readily be provoked by the inattention of state administrators to matters of infrastructure such as sanitation, maintenance of irrigation canals, proper reserves of food and seed, etc.

Exhaustion of natural resources – metals, timber, and oil – also contribute to decline. The Saudi Arab elite cannot be unconcerned about the eventuality of the disappearance of the oil supply. The ancient Mayan state may have collapsed because its agricultural base could no longer support its population.

Decline often leads to increasing oppression, restrictions on thought, on learning and research, because with the decline goes increasing dissatisfaction and grumbling by the masses to which the state, in a desperate attempt to save itself, responds with more prisons, more police, more secret service, more executions. Funds are diverted from productive endeavours to expanding the machinery of oppression. Creativity dries up; new ideas are not forthcoming.

As the state deteriorates opposition groups find a more effective underground and are soon able to organise successful revolts or mount revolutions which overturn the existing state. As Theda Skocpol has pointed out, the Russian Revolution was a success because of the weakness and decline of the Tsarist regime. And if internal usurpers do not take advantage of a decaying state, some other state may take the opportunity to march in. In any case when a state declines sufficiently it is replaced by a new state.

Aside from rise and decline other important processes occur in states. Thus, they may become more authoritarian or more open and a single state may oscillate between the two, as is so common in Latin America – e.g. Mexico, Brazil, Chile.

States may also oscillate between centralisation and decentralisation. Michael Mann offers two cases of a decentralisation process. One is from Southern England (Stonehenge) about the third millennium BCE where "in competition between relatively centralised and decentralised authority, the latter won out ... Authority never did consolidate into a coercive state. Instead it fragmented into lineage and village groups whose elites' own authority was precarious" (64). Apparently we seem to be dealing with a pre- or proto-state situation. In a second example from

Denmark over a much longer period from about 3000BCE to 500BCE, chiefdoms disintegrated in favour of greater egalitarianism with organisation of autonomous local communities on more than one occasion. However, they were eventually followed by the revival of the chiefdom (66). Byock has argued that early Iceland underwent decentralisation in establishing a new society as compared to its homeland, Norway(63 *ff.*).

One might classify the disintegration of the various empires throughout history as a kind of decentralisation. The Roman, Holy Roman, Ottoman, British and any number of other empires all were eventually broken into several smaller entities. But these in turn moved towards their own centralisation. And, indeed, it is well to bear in mind that decentralisation is not a synonym for liberation or freedom. Life can be as nasty and brutish in a decentralised state as in a centralised one.

History seems to provide only slim evidence for any distinguishable decentralisation processes. There are no cases of a society once having been organised as a state reverting to an earlier anarchy. Some have referred to the disintegration of a state such as in present day Somalia as a reversion to anarchy, but this is incorrect. What occurs is a disintegration into what are essentially micro-states – segments dominated by ruling gangs. Like it or not, the general trend has been towards greater political centralisation, to stratification and the state, with only occasional minor 'pulsations' of reaction – slight and temporary reversals of people running off on alternative paths.

Perhaps it is appropriate finally to note that states are rarely diminished by 'revolutions'. Revolutions entail a circulation of elites. One regime is replaced by another. In fact, the revolutionary process often revivifies the state (as with the French and Russian revolutions). Once, at least, there was an attempt to destroy the state by revolution and this was in the unsuccessful attempt by the anarchists of Spain in 1936-1939.

## Types of polity

States may be classified according to their polity or form of government, an early type of which is an oligarchy. Ancient Sumer in southern Mesopotamia had developed around the end of the fourth millennium BCE a number of oligarchic city-states. What kind of system existed before this and specifically how the state arose is not known, but a kind of state administered from temples, that is, religious centres with powerful religious functionaries seem to have been important. Possibly we could surmise, on the basis of what is known about similar situations elsewhere, that the ruling nobility acquired their position through a type of redistribution combined with hierarchy and private property. Ancient Sumerian city states possessed ruling councils. There was an assembly of the elders – the landed nobility – and a lower 'house' of 'men' who were the non-noble free men. There was also a governor who was initially a first among equals, but as conflict between the city-states became more violent he assumed a superior position. He seems in the beginning to have been appointed to a temporary position to deal with a specific military issue and eventually to have acquired a permanent job along with a variety of special privileges. In the end he became a hereditary monarch.

I have said that the Sumerian city-states were initially ruled by an oligarchy, and by this I suggest that the assembly of nobles constituted a small body of a ruling elite and the lower assembly of the non-noble freemen was subordinate to it. Even the latter did not represent a majority of the population since most of the people were servants, slaves and women.

Aside from the assemblies and the governor, another major power block in early Sumer was the temple with its priests and administrative staff. Their economic influence was considerable since the temple, at least in the city of Lagash, owned well over ten percent of the irrigated land and was likely the biggest landlord.

Oligarchies are not an uncommon phenomenon, but as the case of Sumeria shows they can readily become hereditary monarchies.

The second form of government is a theocracy in which god is somehow supposed to rule. There are two kinds of theocracy, one in which it is believed that the ruler is in fact god and another in which it is held that the ruler is god's regent on earth.

Egypt is the best example of the first for here the pharaoh is the god-king and presumably absolute ruler. It is however interesting to note that this did not prevent some pharaohs from being dethroned or murdered. The absolute nature of the Egyptian divine kingship was also rather limited by the fact that Egypt extended for some five hundred miles along the Nile and, while in its day this afforded some efficiency in communication, at the same time that communication was extremely slow. Therefore local administrators, especially in the more remote sections and on the frontier, could practice some considerable autonomy.

Under the pharaoh was a body of chief ministers including a vizier; there were provincial governors, large landlords and temple priests, all of whom together comprised a single elite group. The mass of the population were peasants who were obligated to pay taxes as well as provide labour service – corvee – in the construction of public works (temples, monuments, mortuary structures, palaces, and irrigation canals). They could also be conscripted for military service. Slaves, chiefly war captives, were a minority. With a large supply of peasants, slaves were far less important than they were, for instance, in the southern United States or Brazil.

One of the interesting features which pervaded the long reign of the god-kings of Egypt was the importance of a large number of civil servants who acquired their offices by virtue of their intelligence and education. These scribes were trained in what appears to have been a somewhat informal manner. On assuming office they figured the requirements for public works, reckoned land measurements, calculated taxes and made out the lists for corvee labour. They were an indispensable element in the administration of the country. Apparently the office of scribe was open to common peasants since even the poor endeavoured to have a son trained for the post. According to Barbara Lesko, "even military leaders, significant though they were to the real power of the Egyptian empire, emphasised their education by including 'scribe' among their official titles, and it was as a scribe, rather than an armed fighting man, that the great army commanders had themselves portrayed in their statuary" (17).

The notion of a divine king found expression in some of the pre-colonial states in Sub-Saharan Africa, and in Polynesia so-called chiefs were at least treated as if they were divine. Thus Hawaiian rulers imposed a taboo against anyone touching their person or their belongings, so that violators would be summarily executed.

As was mentioned above, the other form of theocracy makes an individual ruler the regent of god's will on earth. We still have one example of this arrangement, namely the Vatican. The pope speaks for god since he is, in matters of faith and morals, infallible. The Vatican is a most unusual form of state in that it is the smallest sovereign state in the world, yet claims the allegiance of almost as many people as does China. Every member of the Roman Catholic Church has his citizenship in any one of dozens of countries and his 'citizenship' in the Church and thereby his subordination to the Vatican head of state. Obviously this may generate some conflict of interest and the papacy has throughout its history experienced difficulties over this issue with a variety of secular states.

The Islamic caliphates are yet another example of a theocracy where a mortal man is god's agent or direct representative on earth. In Islam god has revealed himself to the prophet Mohammed in the form of the Qur'an, which, except for the first chapter, is believed to be god literally speaking. These words lay out god's plan for a proper society. With the aid of Hadith, the reports of the inspired words and acts of the prophet, along with such devices as analogy and logical reasoning, it is believed that one can draw from the Qur'an all the rules and obligations necessary for the operation of society. Ideally, consequently, there is no need for legislation. The legislation is already provided, derived from these sources and presented in the form of the Shari'a, the law of god. Technically the only function of a ruler is to enforce this law. However in the course of the evolution of the caliphate it was found necessary to make further legislation where a particular issue was not dealt with in the divine law.

In the beginning of the caliphate, during the period referred to by the Sunnis as that of the four rightly-guided caliphs, these rulers were elected by a male assembly. But following this the caliphate became a hereditary position and indeed, as the power and influence of the Abbasid caliphate declined, the caliph became only a figurehead and was eclipsed by a secular vizier. With the dissolution of the Abbasid caliphate, the Ottoman Turkish sultans tried to revive the concept of caliph by adding it to their titles, but it had no more meaning than the title defender of the faith has in modern British royalty. Today, of course, there is no caliph.

Under the caliphates and in most Muslim states to this day a powerful element in the society aside from the ruler has been the body of scholars learned in the holy law. This group – the 'ulama – advised the head of state on legal matters, acted as judges (qadis) in courts, delivered sermons in mosques and taught the university students. As learning in ancient Egypt provided a vehicle for upward mobility so also in the Muslim world scholarship was a means by which even poor and lower class men might rise in status.

It should however not be assumed that the 'ulama had anywhere near the power of the ruler. They did often act as a buffer between the head of state and the ordinary folk, but most frequently had to walk softly. Undoubtedly the military commanders and landed aristocrats were as influential and more so.

Aside from theocracies the relationship between religion and the state has produced such entities as caesaro-papism and varying degrees of divorce or balance between the religious institution and the state. Caesaro-papism is in some respects like theocracy turned on its head, because under it the secular rulers command the religious aspects of life, appoint all the religious functionaries and hold veto power over matters of 'faith and morals' and ritual. This situation was characteristic of Byzantium and one might suppose that Henry VIII introduced this system into England. This has come down to the present day in a much abbreviated form where the Prime Minister of the United Kingdom, whether a member of the Church of England or not, has responsibility for appointing bishops of the church.

Among the more secularly oriented states there are absolute monarchies, democracies and dictatorships. Sometimes we hear of republican states as if they were a distinct form different from any of the above or, more often, equivalent to a democracy. However, in reality, a republic may be any state which is not ruled by a monarch. Republics have frequently been oligarchies as with the Medieval Italian cities or in ancient Rome. They have also been totalitarian dictatorships. In the last days of Mussolini his fascist state was called a republic; Saddam Hussein in Iraq and Hafez al Asad in Syria presided over republics which are quite totalitarian. Numerous republics, including those in Latin America and modern Africa, have at one time or other been dictatorships without being totalitarian. And, of course, the United States calls itself a republic.

In addition, monarchies as well may be quite variant in their form. That is, they may be absolute – a distinct category mentioned above – but other forms of monarchy, sometimes called constitutional monarchies, are democratic. There are also what may be termed decentralised monarchies, the most notable being in Medieval Western Europe when feudalism provided for a monarch whose powers were severely curtailed by a landed aristocracy. The king, a landed aristocrat himself, was a first among equals within the upper class.

In the absolute monarchy presumably no one can challenge the decision of the ruler, who is invariably a hereditary monarch, although in some situations the monarch is elected by a noble elite. The use of the term absolute requires some qualification. The ruler depends upon a group of trusted advisors and is often readily swayed by their opinions. In addition there are court intrigues and the machinations, especially of provincial administrators in more remote areas, which can limit the absolute quality of the monarch. Until modern times the nature of the means of communication and transportation, including the possibilities for surveillance and spying, were such that decrees could be ignored. Thus, the absoluteness of the monarch was further curtailed.

Absolute monarchs buttressed their position by closely identifying themselves with divinity, although they did not profess to be gods. Some came close to assuming they were his divine agents, however. In Europe there developed the notion of the divine right of kings, the ruler was divinely ordained to assume the position of head of state.

Today the absolute monarchy is extremely rare. Saudi Arabia is the largest of those which remain. Five hundred years ago the majority of all states were of this type.

The Renaissance and Reformation in Europe sparked the emergence of democratic governments, although the first such were apparently those in ancient Greece. The Athenian democracy is much referred to, but one may wonder to what extent it was actually more of an oligarchy ruled by an elite of the educated freemen. In any case, like many democracies after it, the majority of the population being slaves or women had no say in the administration of affairs. Technically, a democracy entails the rule by the majority (presumably of adults) and what this has meant is the election of lawmakers – representatives from the electorate – by the populace. Direct democracy in which the populace are invited to assemble and vote on issues is a rare phenomenon limited entirely to a few cases of administration of local village or town affairs. In some New England communities there is still some effort to manage affairs by periodic town meeting, although much power is delegated to, usually three, selectmen. A similar kind of arrangement among Berbers in North Africa differs from the above in that decisions are not by majority vote, but rather by consensus and, therefore, would not fit the democratic image.

After Greece, Iceland and Switzerland can claim to be the oldest European democracies. The American Republic was the first state in most recent times to embark on a political system which professed democratic principles, although the British were also clearly moving towards the same end. For the first four decades of the United States, democracy and majority rule meant that only white, free and property-owning adult males could participate. This amounted to about ten percent of the population. Then, the property restriction was dropped, more than doubling the voters. The end of slavery by 1865 opened the door for non-white participation, but this was only very slowly achieved. Women's suffrage did not appear until after World War One, while most blacks remained disenfranchised for nearly another half century thereafter.

Granted that in most so-called democracies today there is universal suffrage, in most elections only fifty to sixty percent consider it worthwhile to vote. In addition, except in a few European states where there is some kind of proportional representation, the winner of an election is the one who receives the largest number of votes, not the one with the majority of votes. Consequently, taking these factors into consideration, it is a rare event that any representative to any parliament is elected and supported by a majority of eligible voters. It is not uncommon for a victorious candidate to have the support of only twenty percent of the electorate. On top of this, what one is voting for is a representative; there is no direct participation and most of these representatives are alleged to speak for one hundred thousand up to five hundred thousand people. This I would suggest is not exactly what most people have in mind when they speak of democracy.

Constitutional monarchies are today fully in the democratic camp because the monarch holds only a ceremonial position and legislative powers are vested in an elected body. Having said this, there are certainly some extreme circumstances – such as if there were a popularly elected communist or revolutionary anti-monarchist government – which would provoke some kind of coup. Finally, there are what might be called quasi-constitutional monarchies where the monarch exercises great power, although it does not reach an absolute status. Morocco and Jordan are examples.

The most recent form of polity is the totalitarian state, e.g. Nazi Germany or Stalinist USSR. The reason this type is very modern is that for any kind of total control of the citizenry to occur requires technology which has only been invented in this century. A proper totalitarian state requires the most sophisticated surveillance devices; with new technologies and the application of psychology, the most exquisite forms of torture are introduced. More jails and concentration camps are required; police, especially secret police and informants, must be added. All citizens and children are encouraged to be informants so that witch-hunts are perpetual. As in all states, the young are trained to be loyal and obedient servants of the state and its leader, but in the totalitarian state this becomes an obsession. There are periodic purges as 'disloyal' state officials are marched off to execution. The press, radio, television, motion pictures – all forms of communication – fall under strict state management. Paranoia and terror reign. The state is all.

\*   \*   \*

In the evolution of the state over its five to six thousand year history there have been two clear trends. One has been a movement from authoritarian theocracies and absolute monarchies to the appearance of liberal democracy. The second trend has been a movement towards ever more authoritarian governments, culminating in the totalitarian state. With modern technology it is at last possible to create a truly absolute totalitarian state.

I would argue that the long sweep of history demonstrates that the state is an inherently despotic institution. The vast majority of states have been tyrannies according to anyone's criteria. It will be pointed out, however, that today we have more democracies than ever before, that perhaps half of modern states would fit somehow into such a category. Therefore, it is held things are looking up; the world is becoming more liberal, more free.

But consider the reality of the democratic ideal: the sanctity of majority vote. While the absolute monarchy and the totalitarian state place their trust in a single leader, democracy elevates the majority decision of the populace to a divine status, even though it rarely ever actually implements it. In the democratic state the election of rulers by alleged majority vote is a subterfuge which helps individuals to believe that they control the situation. They are selecting persons to do a task for them and they have no guarantee that it will be carried out as they desired. They are abdicating to these persons, granting them the right to impose their own wills by threat of force. Electing individuals to public office is like being given a limited choice of your oppressors.

We frequently hear the refrain: if you don't vote you have no right to complain. Such an argument makes the false assumption that an election provides real choices. But more so, it falsely assumes the legitimacy of the process itself: that an individual is required to delegate authority to an arbitrarily chosen few, or that an individual is required to elect his or her own jailers. Above all, there is the fundamental moral question about the sanctity of the majority. Democracy, in its advocacy of majority rule, attempts to provide an alternative to the rule of one, but it often replaces that kind of dictatorship by one of the majority or, most commonly, of the plurality. It assumes that right and wrong, that morality, can be determined by a majority of those who bother to vote. Ibsen's *Enemy of the People* is a vivid dramatisation of some of the consequences of relying upon majorities. Yet even aside from the fact that minorities might know better, or have right on their side, there remains the truth that the majority compels the minority to conform.

No democracy has freed itself from rule by the well-to-do anymore than it has freed itself from the division between the ruler and the ruled. Marx's remark that the state is the executive committee of the capitalist class has relevance for the democratic state. That is, at the very least, no democracy has jeopardised the role of business enterprise. Only the wealthy and well off can afford to launch viable campaigns for public office and to assume such positions. Change in government in a democracy is a circulation from one elite group to another. Parliamentary democracies are essentially oligarchies in which the populace is led to believe that it delegates all its authority to members of parliament to do as they think best. In a democracy just as in a totalitarian state it is not possible to withhold from a decision of the state. Whether you like it or not you are a subject of the state. As the American Civil War demonstrated no segment may secede. Democracies are no less enthusiasts of nationalist flag waving, patriotic mumbo jumbo, and militarism than any other kind of state. Further, the judiciary is such that a judge has few limits to his authority. Democracy provides a more benign and subtle form of despotism, the totalitarian state is more crass, more monstrous – more frank.

## Archaic and modern states

Whether democratic, theocratic or totalitarian all states share basic common features. At the same time it has been suggested that there are significant differences between the modern state and those of an earlier time. The dividing line between archaic and modern states seems to be in the late Medieval period in Europe.

In the modern state there is a strong nationalistic spirit, a glorification of the nation. This does not occur in the archaic state where much of the populace is at most hardly aware of their belonging to a nation, identifying rather with a local village or at best a province or tribe.

The modern state maintains numerous ministries and an enormous bureaucracy. Up to ten percent of the working population may be employed by the state in one form or another. The archaic state has few ministries and the bureaucracy is minimal, even non-existent in some cases. Considerably less than one percent of workers would be employed by the state.

The modern state devotes a considerable amount of its expenditure and its bureaucracy to the provision of social services. Modern states tend to become welfare states. The archaic state provides no social services; expenditures are divided between those for a military establishment and war and those for the maintenance of a royal entourage.

There is a strong tendency for modern states to build large standing armies and to institute compulsory military training for all young men. In the archaic state standing armies are minimal and, when the state is in need of cannon fodder, villages are raided to impress young men into the military.

Boundaries between modern states are clear and unambiguous and within the last century they have been increasingly more difficult to cross. This contrasts with the archaic state.

The modern state is more effective in its control of the populace. Here there is a direct correlation with increasing technological sophistication which brings with it more efficient methods for surveillance and data collection. While the archaic state might claim a monopoly on the use of violence within its sovereign borders, in fact it finds itself faced with continual, often successful, challenges to this claim. Sometimes the opposition is in the form of another institution. Thus, early Medieval Europe states found a formidable opponent in the church. Nobles frequently challenged the power of the king.

# Chapter 3

# The Origin of the State

The seeds of the state have been sown in every human society. Yet as we have seen in Chapter 1 only a very few of these seeds have ever come to fruition. Most states have been created by being imposed on a people or as a defensive mechanism to allow for better interaction with an already existent state. It is the purpose of this chapter to investigate how the state emerges primarily as a pristine or autochthonous entity. First let us consider some of these seeds of statism as they appear in what have been called egalitarian and rank type societies and why they do not mature.

Perhaps the overwhelming majority of so-called egalitarian societies, that is those which lack a state and government and presumably grant some equality for adult males, place a great deal of dependence upon elder men. This patriarchal system, it might be argued, does have a certain rationality in that it is the elders who have lived the longest and so could be expected to have the most experience in living and, hence, wisdom. But it is irrational in that it assumes that those in the 'elder' status are automatically always superior, and it also assumes that only males belong to it.

By its nature this 'old man' syndrome alone cannot perpetuate an elite power as a dynasty and so create a state. A man assumes power in this kind of society as an older person and retains it for a few short years at which time he must yield to new persons who were his subordinates. Indeed, in an age-graded society such as the West African Tiv, a man assumes leadership for a short span of a decade, when he must retire to inactivity and now find himself in a social setting where those who were his subordinates are now leaders. Another reason patriarchy in this sort of setting will not lead to government *per se* is that the entire system is intimately attached to kinship. Patriarchs or elders are grandfathers of some kind. One is not obligated to obey those one does not address with a kin term.

Henry Maine in his *Ancient Law* recognised two polar types of society. One was the ancient tribal system and the other the state which evolved out of the tribal. The first of these was based on kinship ties, in which every member believed he was related to all others in the group. Members obeyed a head man, not as a ruler of a state, but as a senior kinsman, as head of a family, a father. Early societies were primarily of this type and in the course of time some evolved into societies with a different basis of membership – that of territory. 'Local contiguity' rather than kinship became the basis for deciding the ultimate authority. Such a society entails a government and a state. Gluckman has noted that Maine meant to stress that the 'revolution' in social order comes about when dwelling in a certain territory was sufficient to grant citizenship without having to create a kinship tie either by marriage, adoption or through inventing a genealogical connection. "The alteration comes when a kinship idiom to express political association is no longer demanded" (86). One might say then that kinship is opposed to the state.

Hocart has argued that the earliest government-like functions were assumed by ritual specialists, some of whom, eventually, became fully-fledged rulers of states as part of a general process of increasing specialisation in the division of labour. We have already noted a process of this kind in connection with the first states. It is evident that power derived from the possession of knowledge – and usually religious knowledge – is often highly significant in the social dynamics of small societies. The Australian elder adds to his power by his control of esoteric ceremonial knowledge, the Inuit shaman by his control of curing techniques and the manipulation of the dark arts. The Nuer leopard skin chief has the power to curse, as do the elders and rainmakers among the Lugbara. The foundation and legitimacy of the Anuak chief's and Shilluk 'king's' role rest entirely in its ritual and supernatural significance. Economic factors are hardly the only sources of power. Indeed we see this today when technicians and other specialists can command great influence, not because of their wealth, but because of their knowledge. Functionaries with knowledge as well as individuals who assume mediator positions in stateless societies are often entitled to invoke sanctions which border on the legal.

In slightly more rank ordered societies where one has the so-called Big Man phenomenon one also finds the germ of state development. In New Guinea this leader acquires a body of clients which he is able in some cases to command. Mair has contended that the foundation of a state could be in this development by a leader of a dependent and loyal body of supporters. Slightly different is the individual among the Inuit who is able to lord it over a community by his own physical force or use of dreaded supernatural powers.

With the Big Man, anarchy can degenerate into tyranny. What sometimes occurs may be seen as an abortive attempt to introduce a governmental-state system. It is a failure in part because there is an ambivalence within the community towards authority, so that if established it regularly inspires rebellion and the Big Man who tries to be the bully is most often murdered. Thus, the situation returns to an acephalous or anarchic condition.

Why don't all these societies ridden with their domineering elders, their Big Men, their shamans and powerful mediators readily become states with governments? Perhaps the main reason is that none of these individuals have any adequate ideological, economic, technological or organisational base. They are limited by the productive capability of any dependents they might acquire and this is inhibited by lack of a more complex technology. Nor can one expect to control extensive territories with the available, very simple methods of communication and transportation. At the same time any power is maintained and extended only through a network of personal contacts. There is no organisation of loyal bureaucrats to sustain a realm. The difference between king and Big Man is fundamental according to Harold Schneider: kings receive tribute and submission; Big Men must rely on support. "Rather than being a stage in the evolution of government, the state, or rather the monarchy, is but a point on one end of a spectrum whose other end is stateless societies containing only big men" (Schneider, 207).

Materialist explanations have emphasised the economic, technological and organisational factors mentioned above. They have ignored the crucial ideological element. In stateless societies no adequate ideology of superiority/inferiority has been developed. Over and over again one may note that the inhabitants of such communities will not tolerate what seems to be oppression and the creation of a permanent elite. Tough guys are murdered. Pierre Clastres' thesis in *Society Against the State* is that among the Amazonian tribes the chief is severely curtailed and made a servant rather than a ruler because he has violated the rules of reciprocity. As Max Weber noted, a particular social system will not develop unless, among other things, it also has an adequate ideology. An ideology amenable to state development is one which assumes the legitimacy of dominance by a few superiors over a mass of inferiors.

## Significant elements of state development

In the previous discussion several factors which seem to be essential for state development have been briefly alluded to. Now we must deal with each of these issues and others not thus far mentioned. But, first, it is important to recognise that any social phenomenon is an emergent from the interaction of a variety of factors. It is a configuration of parts, the configuration being different from but not more than the sum of the parts. Monocausality is an error and at best a simplistic attempt at explanation. Most of the theories of state origin, some of which will be dealt with below, have sought to reduce the explanation of the state, and other institutions as well, to a single cause which means they have overlooked the significance of other things.

Ronald Cohen has written: "there is no clear cut or simple set of causal statements that explains the phenomenon of state formation ... The formation of states is a funnel-like progression of interactions in which a variety of pre-state systems responding to different determinants of change are forced by otherwise unresolvable conflicts to choose additional and more complex levels of political hierarchy." Once this is achieved there occurs a convergence of forms towards the early state (142). Pre-state systems are placed on the track towards the state if they have already an existent hierarchy and there are attempts by some elite to achieve and maintain power and domination. When an attempt is successful one has a state or, put another way, the state is born when an elite can claim for itself a monopoly on the use of violence and can institute legal sanctions as defined in chapter 1. The hierarchy is built upon a number of factors. The significant elements in state development are, then:

1. Population

2. Sedentary settlement

3. Horticulture/agriculture

4. Redistribution

5. Military organisation

6. Secondary significance of kinship

7. Trading

8. Specialised division of labour

9. Individual property and control of resources

10. Hierarchic social order

11. Ideology of superiority/inferiority

## Population

A hunting-gathering band of a few dozen members could never constitute a state simply because it lacks the necessary manpower and resources. However, earliest Sumerian city-states survived with a few thousand inhabitants. Each was able to do so because it was about the same size as all the other states and they were all eventually consolidated into a single Sumerian state under Sargon I. The Athenian city-state as well had but several thousand inhabitants, but initially it too competed with entities of about the same size. Soon it was forced to form coalitions to deal with external conflicts and, finally, like the Sumerian city-states, it disappeared in an empire.

In modern times it has already been noted that there are a great number of what may be called micro-states. A few of these, too, have less than thirty thousand inhabitants. Thus, there is Tuvalu with a bare ten square miles and less than ten thousand people, or Nauru with eight square miles and about ten thousand residents. Such odd entities are hardly viable states and are thoroughly dependent upon major states for survival; indeed, they exist out of the grace of the larger states. As with most of the smaller states, they exist in a neo-colonialist atmosphere. The larger, mightier polities do not have to have direct control of these societies in the form of colonies. They may readily tolerate their questionable sovereignty, but control their economies and insure by subtle and indirect means that their politics do not become too unacceptable. On the other hand, these tiny entities may not be worth bothering about. Hitler never bothered with Andorra or Liechtenstein, and San Marino eventually adopted an independent fascist government during Mussolini's years.

To be viable a state must have a certain minimal size and that depends upon the particular social milieu within which it is located. In Medieval Europe a state with a million inhabitants would have been quite effective, other considerations being equal.

Today this would be questionable.

Geographic size may be less important than population, although clearly the importance and viability of sovereign states with a bare few square miles are questionable. At the same time the substantial city-state of Singapore with three million people and 239 square miles seems to manoeuvre reasonably well in the halls of power. It is apparent, however, that the larger the territory one has, the more self-sustaining the economy can be and the potential for resources is likewise greater.

Carniero has argued that population growth is a major impetus for state creation. A people may reside in an area exploiting its agricultural potential, resulting in population increase and demands or pressures for more arable lands. Eventually this provokes aggression and conquest of other areas and peoples and, in order to achieve success in such an enterprise, necessitates armies which are organised by states. Population and conquest are here seen as the two motivations for state creation. But they are in fact only two pieces of a much more complex puzzle. The state does not rise like a phoenix out of an enlarged and predatory population alone. Most of the factors mentioned later in this chapter are ignored.

We may suppose that populations increased towards the end of the Paleolithic and that this was largely caused by a process in which new technology appeared, including the bow and arrow, more sophisticated stone tools, the domestication of the dog, and improved clothing and housing. These changes meant that the age of marriage could be lowered, spacing of children reduced, and abortion and infanticide decreased, culminating in further population increases and thus a search for improved sources of food.

Researchers believe that humans no doubt understood the process of plant and animal reproduction and growth thousands of years before actually domesticating such things as wheat, barley, pulses and sheep. As hunter-gatherers they were free of the more arduous tasks which would be associated with cultivation. But population increases would eventually challenge their sources of food. In addition climatic changes occurring at the end of the last Ice Age may have threatened traditionally exploited wild plants and game. Horticulture would have been a reasonable resolution of the situation. There is, however, no reason to believe that in every case there should soon arise an absolute limit to available arable land and a necessity to expand by military aggression. States in Egypt and Sumer did not arise because of pressure for arable land. Early horticultural societies would also have still no little dependence upon gathering and hunting to supplement their supplies. Finally, a sometimes fashionable explanation for the spread of inventions and peoples has been migration. Rather than conquest a people might merely move to a more profitable location: no need for conquest or the state.

## Sedentarism

All states with few exceptions have arisen out of sedentary populations. This is clearly so with both the earliest states of the Old and the New World: Sumeria, Egypt, India, China, Mexico and Peru. The only exceptions to this rule have been those states created by pastoral nomads, such as the Huns and the Mongols and early Turks. These were all, however, secondary states created on the model of already existing states and in response to them. They have already been mentioned in Chapter 2. But as far as sedentarism is concerned it is necessary to point out that once these nomads adopted the state they became sedentary. In addition it must be borne in mind that the nomadism of pastoralists is not the nomadism of hunter-gatherers. No hunting-gathering nomad group could ever produce a state, if only because it lacks the adequate resources and infrastructure. Pastoralists, on the other hand, possess great wealth in their herds and in their ancillary, often predatory, activities. They possess, as has been said, a walking larder.

As we have noted above Ibn Khaldun developed a theory of state development based on the proposition that pastoral nomads invade and take over an already decaying city to establish their own new state. But, observe that both the sedentary community and the state already exist independent of any nomads.

Why is sedentarism fundamental to state development? States require some concentration of population wherein there is some specialisation of labour; they require centres for administration and extensive horticulture or agriculture. (Pastoralists engage in a bit of indifferent cultivation, but nearly all of them are dependent upon sedentary farmers for part of their food.)

The most concentrated type of sedentary life is that of the city. As in almost all cases, where you find the city you will find the state. Polynesian states and the earliest Mayans do not seem to have had true cities, but cities seem to be integral elements of states and they are clear signs of civilisation. Not only are they administrative centres, they are industrial and craft centres and the important sites for trade. Perhaps a majority of cities have arisen as market places; others have appeared as objects of religious pilgrimage or as capitals of states or military centres. Perhaps sedentarism, and particularly urban life, is so universal in state development because it provides the sense of permanence and stability so important in the wielding of power.

But sedentarism, especially the concentration of cities, brings with it grossly unsanitary conditions, disease and epidemics. Means of disposal of garbage and wastes are minimal and livestock roam the streets and alleys. Nomadism provides a far healthier environment since one can set up camp and remain in a location until the rubbish becomes too much of a nuisance. At which time one can move to another location.

# Horticulture/agriculture

A third minimal requirement for the creation of a state is the cultivation of domesticated plants and primary dependence upon them as a source of food. Again, all of the pristine centres of the state were characterised by the maintenance of large cultivated areas. Initially this was by digging stick and hoe involving large gardens, technically, horticulture. In the Ancient Near East the use of domesticated draft animals – oxen and later donkeys, mules and camels – along with the plough and wheeled vehicles arose almost coterminously with the state. The employment of such power, plus the extensive cultivation of fields, distinguishes agriculture from horticulture. In Mexico and Peru the early states remained dependent upon the latter engaging in very intensive gardening. They also contrasted with the Old World in paying little attention to animal husbandry. In Peru they kept llamas as pack animals and for their wool, while in the Eastern Hemisphere a host of animals were eventually domesticated for meat, milk, wool and draught. Horses and mules pulled chariots which were the formidable tanks of the ancient Eastern states.

In the East as well pastoralism became an important adjunct specialisation, exploiting the vast non-arable and arid lands. For most of Asia and North Africa cultivation depended upon irrigation. All of the original ancient states arose on river banks: Sumer on the Tigris and Euphrates, Egypt on the Nile, India (Pakistan) on the Indus, and China on the Yellow River. This correlation led Karl Wittfogel to develop a technological determinist thesis concerning the origins of ancient states in Egypt and Asia. These were for him 'hydraulic civilisations' which commenced on the banks of great rivers. They were the source of elaborate artificial irrigation works which depended on the organisation of centralised mechanisms for control, hence engendering the development of the state as manager.

Paul Wheatley reviewed the evidence for Wittfogel's theory in regard to China and found it wanting (292 *ff.*). In China the large-scale hydraulic works were intended mainly for transportation rather than agriculture. Furthermore, they were not the product of centralised government except where they were specific military ventures. Rather, they were made and maintained by local or regional groups. For Mesopotamia, Robert Adams has written that "there is nothing to suggest that the rise of dynastic authority in northern Mesopotamia was linked to the administration requirements of a major canal system" (Kraeling and Adams, 281). The Mesopotamian walled city-state arose considerably before any large-scale irrigation and must therefore have other causes. In the Andean region as well urban development occurred first, and only sometime later did major irrigation canals appear. Canals associated with the Nile were primarily built for the transportation of stone for pyramid building and other public works or for draining swamps. Egyptian sources give no indication of a role for irrigation canals in administration. If such technology were crucial for the creation of the Egyptian state one would expect otherwise. Hoffman, on the other hand, suggests that Wittfogel's theory may not be totally in error, rather it is 'overstated'. "Egyptian irrigation technology was never as extensive or as complex as that of Mesopotamia or China, revolving mainly about basins that evened out the effects of the annual inundation ... hydraulic networks in Egypt were localised, not rambling linear affairs like their Mesopotamian counterparts; hence any political ramifications that irrigation had would have been restricted to a small geographical area." If we go back to the later pre-dynastic period "when Upper Egypt was apparently divided into a number of regional political units and consider the symbolic importance attached to irrigation and hydraulic projects by monarchs like Scorpion and later First Dynasty pharaohs ... then it is logical to suppose that the manipulation of irrigation technology, at least, required the patronage of a big man on a local level and the skills he or his clients possessed" (Hoffman, 314-316).

In more recent times, several peoples living on the island of Luzon in the Philippines have had both highly decentralised anarchic political structures and rather complex systems of rice irrigation. It would appear that with irrigation systems it is not that they demand a centralised, hierarchical control in the form of state management. It is that they require coordination of some kind – a coordination which can be achieved through a variety of different means, but, given what has been said above, that coordination is most commonly a matter of very local control.

There are several reasons why a complex horticulture or agriculture is fundamental to state development. Early gardening was not much more productive or efficient than gathering and hunting, but as people became more dependent upon domesticated plants and animals, yields increased because of the effort in improving seed and agricultural techniques. Not only did this allow for much larger populations, but it also permitted a few individuals to become specialists in given tasks and not be engaged in the production of their food. What is more, it laid the groundwork for a tiny minority to become a leisure class of administrators and aristocrats.

The growing of crops and domesticated animals further gave some security to the food supply. With the creation of a variety of storage techniques there could ordinarily be sufficient food for a year until the next harvest. The dependence upon hunting wild game in the pre-agricultural condition was a much more risky business. On the other hand, horticulture and agriculture were not always that secure. Especially with the appearance of monoculture, in which large fields were devoted to a single crop, there was the periodic threat of that crop being totally destroyed by insect infestation or epidemic disease. The dependence upon artificial irrigation meant that there would be years in which the river did not supply a sufficient amount of water or others in which it produced too much. Any of these conditions could lead to food shortages and sometimes to massive famine.

A dependence upon domesticated plants and animals as well as irrigation greatly enhanced land and livestock values. Particularly once kinship was no longer the basis for having rights to land, some individuals were able to acquire more land than others. Some became Big Men through their ability to talk and manipulate others, through supernatural powers, through overt force or their ability to gather a body of clients in large part by making the less successful indebted to them. The Big Men became then the landlords; agriculture reinforced hierarchy.

Agriculture also produced peasants – the largest single segment of humanity for the last five thousand years. Although the peasant life is not totally black and depressing, everyone will agree that it has been characterised by poverty, disease and insecurity. Work as a pejorative was invented with peasantry. Not only does the peasant work long hours, but the labour is back breaking and mostly drudgery. The peasant is continually harassed by his lord. Thousands of years of subservience have sought to train a body of duly obedient servants, necessary ingredients for any state. It has been hypothesised that the slave mentality is further maintained by the fact that the more intelligent and those who do not fully learn subservience in the peasant community are siphoned off by migration to the towns, where any rebellious spirit can be sublimated by other challenges.

## Redistribution

There are three different kinds of economic exchange: reciprocity, redistribution and the market. Reciprocity is universal in human societies and the oldest method of exchange. It is a kind of gift giving in which one provides a product or a service for another on the, usually implicit, understanding that there will be a return of something of equivalent value in the future by the recipient. Reciprocity may be immediate or delayed. It is quite likely that the immediate reciprocity is widespread among mammal species. For instance horses and apes groom one another. Humans, too, resort to reciprocity of this type, but with their greater mental capability they can readily remember various details which allows them to indulge in delayed reciprocity. George recalls that two years ago Stanley contributed $100 to the marriage of George's daughter, Now Stanley requires repairs on his house and George is obligated to contribute to the repairs in an equivalent fashion. Even in present day market dominated society reciprocity survives. Last year my sister sent me a Christmas gift and so I will duly send her one again this year in anticipation that she will do the same. Among other things reciprocity stresses that there are no free gifts. It is also a method of exchange between equals – one does not require some kind of hierarchical arrangement.

Redistribution does require hierarchy, at least in some minimal form. It requires several individuals to assemble some kind of wealth in one location and one person is assigned the responsibility for redistributing this wealth. Again, as with reciprocity, there is the appearance of gift giving, especially in its simplest expression.

The problem with the redistribution concept has been that it is somewhat of an umbrella term, covering a wide variety of activities. Thus, in New Guinea a Big Man loans out piglets to his neighbours and when they are grown he calls for contributions to a feast which he sponsors and acquires prestige as a result. Potlatching was a common celebration among the American Indians of the Northwest Coast. A Big Man's kinsmen were expected to supply food and other goods for a major feast or potlatch, the climax of which involved the distribution of 'gifts' to the assembled guests by the Big Man. From this he not only earned prestige, but also acquired important titles and his prestige was especially enhanced if he could outdo a rival in 'gift' giving – if he could 'flatten' an opponent.

With the Near Eastern archaic states such as Egypt, the pattern of redistribution was more complex. Peasants were expected to deposit part of their crop in a local storehouse. In Egypt a great number of storehouses were created by the state throughout the country and what was not consumed in a locality was sent on to central depositories at the royal court. While in New Guinea and in the Northwest Coast the redistribution serviced a general populace, in the Near East it benefited primarily aristocrats, priests and the military, functioning as a means of collecting tribute for their benefit. There, as well, it was the chief type of economic exchange.

For the past several hundred years it has declined in favour of market arrangements. Nevertheless, redistribution persists as the means by which the state acquires its operating funds, in the form of taxation. Modern states extract part of the wealth of every citizen and redistribute it. Part goes to support an enormous bureaucracy, part for a military establishment; another part provides subsidies to wealthy corporations, while, especially in the so-called welfare state, no small amount is diverted to health, welfare and education of the common folk. Thus, we have three different kinds of redistribution systems. One is essentially an elaborate feasting and is extremely close to reciprocity. A second provides for centralised storehouses and siphons the wealth off to a dominant minority, the wealth having been appropriated from the labour of the poor. In the third the state collects taxes from the rich and the poor and re-circulates the money to various groups. Until a century ago most of it went to the military and administrative branches of the government, including large sums to a royal family. In recent times more has been returned to the lower echelons, because, one might suggest, governments have learned that it is easier and less expensive in keeping the peace if one can ensure a few crumbs to the hoi polloi.

Today market arrangements dominate world economic exchange, but they were of little or no importance in ancient society. Goods circulated through reciprocity and redistribution and it is to the elaboration of the latter that entails a major impetus to state formation. As has been noted, redistribution, requires a redistributing agent and, hence, at least a minimal hierarchy. Such a figure, then, has great power over the use of resources and can thereby extend his influence and eventually with the combination of other appropriate factors, all of which are being covered in this essay, is able to elevate himself into a position as ruler. This redistribution which is essentially an elaborate feasting device would, however, lack most of the attendant factors which would permit such a development. The appropriate redistribution system would only be a complex one based at a minimum upon horticulture, hierarchy, and a larger population.

## Military organisation

As was observed above Robert Carniero finds the origin of the state in population expansion and conquest. Others have singled out conquest alone as the source of the state. Oppenheimer saw in the expansion of one group to conquer another the creation of an apparatus aimed at maintaining domination. But the several examples he presents are of social entities which were already states when they commenced expansion. This cuts to the heart of the problem with this monocausal explanation.

All animals engage from time to time in intra-species fights. Yet the deliberate attempt to kill an opponent is more characteristic of humans. Among other animals one or both combatants may be killed by accident, not so much by design or intent, although in cases of overcrowding fights do lead to killing. Ordinarily among animals a losing combatant runs away or performs an instinctive ritual of submission which triggers an inhibiting reaction in the victor so that he no longer pursues his aggressive behaviour.

Humans apparently lack any genetically programmed inhibitors that restrain a combatant from killing his opponent. What is controlled by instinctive ritual among animals is restrained by cultural regulation among humans. 'Thou shalt not kill' is a commandment with some degree of validity in every human community. It is not always effective. Not only do individuals engage in hostilities in which there is a deliberate attempt to kill an opponent, but in every human society group endeavours of this kind occur as well. So it is argued warfare is a natural part of human behaviour.

I would argue that warfare is not a half dozen men taking off to raid or engage an equivalent group in another camp. Inter-group hostilities are of varying kinds, such that feuding and small raids can hardly be placed in the same category with warfare. Warfare possesses distinct characteristics which make it qualitatively and quantitatively different from other types of lethal combat. It is different in terms of both the aims and organisation.

A war aims at conquest, that is, a warring party seeks to capture and control the lands, wealth and people of another group. The feuding and raiding which constitute the group hostilities in most human societies lack such aims. The intentions of the feud or raid are much more modest – to even a score, to steal livestock, to abduct women, or, on rare occasions to acquire territory. There are no motives to subdue an opponent or absorb his group. In the feud once a member of one side has been killed or maimed a revenge attack can be expected in which a member of the guilty party will be killed or maimed. On the achievement of this mission the aggressors return home to await retaliation or a proposal for mediation.

The organisation of warfare is vastly more complex than other forms of group hostility. Wars are fought with armies and similar military forces. There are large numbers of men organised according to a chain of command and a division of labour. There are no democratic armies, since there are always some individuals who give orders to others who are expected to obey without question. Occasionally, an army falls into disarray because those at the top cannot agree, but armies are clearly distinguished by the fact that not only do those at the bottom do all the dirty work and face all the danger, but they take all the orders and give none at all. In addition, in a military force the chain of command is quite explicit and obvious to everyone. It is never ambiguous.

In feuding and raiding groups there is invariably no chain of command or, if it does exist, it is a reflection of pre-established relations among the combatants. There may be deference to a senior kinsman or one who has a reputation as a great warrior. Fighting is often quite individualistic with participants each 'doing his own thing'.

Not only are there commanders and the commanded in warfare, but some of the latter may be assigned to actual fighting, others to providing supplies to the fighters, some to repair materiel, yet others to gathering intelligence, to reconnaissance or to tending the wounded. And in each of these categories there is invariably a further refinement in the division of labour.

Warfare requires at least a few semi or full professionals and, for those who are neither, some kind of minimal training is involved. Warfare depends as well on tactics, that is, the organisation and plans for battle, the deployment of troops and the arrangement of the most efficient way in which to achieve a precise goal. Feuds and raids have no professionals and tactics are minimal.

Because warfare entails the mobilisation of substantial numbers of men and supplies, it demands a complex and large organisation which can mount and maintain it. War technology is very expensive even in ancient times where it took substantial wealth to maintain war horses and their gear or chariots and their teams. This is why it is that true warfare seems only to appear with the advent of the state – a substantial predatory structure with the power to command adequate resources. Further, as we have already said, an army is based on unquestioned obedience to command. Such a condition can be associated with a kinship relation or with state management. Thus one may say that army discipline means that some kind of state structure has already been instituted since it has nothing to do with kinship.

Warfare is also the health of the state as Randolph Bourne said. As has already been observed in these pages a state is based upon violence and a concentration of power into a few hands enforcing that power through violence or the threat of it. Throughout history we may note that where there is a vigorous state there is inevitably an orientation towards war. War invigorates the state. It reinforces the power and the glory of the state and maintains and extends its sovereign borders. As all states compete with one another, victory in the competition depends ultimately upon war and the threat of war.

It is interesting and ironic that anarchists and militarists both converge in recognising the significance of violence to the life of the state, although they do so for entirely opposite motivations. Machiavelli recognised force and fraud as the obvious central mechanisms for the success of the state. Von Treitschke, the German historian who was an admirer of Frederick the Great, observed that "without war no State could be. All those we know of arose through war and the protection of their members by armed force remains their primary and essential task. War, therefore, will endure to the end of history as long as there is a multiplicity of States ... the blind worshipper of an eternal peace falls into the error of isolating the state, or dreams of one which is universal, which we have already seen to be at variance with reason" since a state always means one among states and thus opposed to others (38). "Submission is what the State primarily requires ... its very essence is the accomplishment of its will."(14). "The State is no Academy of Arts, still less is it a Stock Exchange; it is Power ..."(242). Gaetano Mosca observed "With good reason did Machiavelli put into the mouth of Cosimo dei Medici that much quoted remark, that states are not ruled with prayer-books" (450). The pioneer anthropologist, Edward B. Tylor wrote in his *Anthropology*, "a constitutional government whether called republic or kingdom, is an arrangement by which the nation governs itself by means of the machinery of a military despotism" (156).

Nietzsche, who contrary to popular opinion was no friend of the state, noted its predatory nature: "The State (is) unmorality organised ... the will to war, to conquest and revenge ..." As a predator the state attempts to become larger and larger, ever expanding its sphere of influence and subjugation at the expense of weaker states. The course of time leads most states to opt out of the conflict and resign themselves to becoming satellites of larger states, realising they cannot effectively compete. It is also true that the giant states may not always seek to gobble up weaker ones, because they find it better for their own interests to keep such states as ostensibly independent entities. Thus, in the modern world, we have super powers which are in the midst of the struggle for expansion, although as I write there is now the unusual circumstance of only one super power – the United States.

Those who advocate a conquest or militarist explanation for state origin are not entirely wrong. Rather than saying warfare and conquest precede the state, I would suggest that the two work in tandem, both evolving together and feeding each other. One thing is certain, and that is in the game of statecraft and international politics no state can expect to achieve importance and prestige unless it does have a good army and pursues the road to dominance.

The seeds for an army and any consequent warfare are to be found in the body of clients some Big Man at the centre of a complex redistribution system can cajole, deceive and manipulate.

## The secondary significance of kinship

The state is a very jealous god. It cannot tolerate competition. Before the appearance of the state the glue which held society together was kinship. The family and secondary kin groupings were paramount demanding prior obligations over all else. As the elements of state formation achieved increasing pre-eminence, the role of kinship was eclipsed. As Maine argued, with the state, place of residence overrode kinship ties.

Within a few millennia prior to the emergence of the state in the Near East, or at a time coterminous with that development, numerous fundamental innovations had occurred. Not only had there been the domestication of numerous plants and animals, but animals were employed for draught purposes; yoking and harnessing devices, copper and other metallurgies, pottery, irrigation, the plough, the looms, more sophisticated methods for measurement, writing, among other inventions, all appeared. Manufacturing and using such items required some training. This in turn provoked the rise of specialisation in labour which was also made possible because agriculture had become sufficiently efficient that it could support a minority of the population as non-food producers. Populations increased and there was a greater movement and mixing of different peoples. Consequently, there came to exist a rather heterogeneous population that was not related by kinship, residing in congested areas like cities. The different occupational specialists had their own interests: conflicts among groups arose which could not be settled by ordinary kinship mechanisms since so many of those involved were unrelated.

Into this situation the state appears to make residence the basis for control. Some Big Man, some pre-eminent, ranking person with adequate resources and clientele marches onto the scene.

It has also been proposed that some people may become so tired from internal fighting that they acquiesce to the rule of a noted and respected mediator, although I have not found any specific case of this in the literature except the one given by Southall in which a non-Alur people invited Alur chiefs to come to judge and rule them. These Alur (who live in East Africa) presumably had "rain-making and conflict resolving powers" (Southall).

One of the main arguments for the state has been an 'integrative' one which largely follows the view that the state is necessary to maintain order in a highly heterogeneous, densely populated situation. But this theory overlooks at least two important points. It ignores the possibility of alternative approaches. For example, all kinds of voluntary organisations exist composed of a variety of different peoples and they all manage to avoid descending into chaos and violence.* Even the inculcation of ethical standards acts as a strong restraining force. The vast majority of people do not kill and maim because of the presence of the police, but because they have been trained that killing is a 'mortal sin'.

The second problem with the integration theory is that it overlooks the ulterior motives of the would-be heads of state. Obviously there are many individuals who are members of parliaments, governors of states, etc., who honestly believe they have a genuine concern for the public welfare. They believe they can use the state to achieve the good life. Consequently some improvements may occur. But in the end their sincere, yet naive, efforts are overridden by obligations to defend the state and enforce the law. Other politicians are clearly more crass, believing that the welfare of General Motors is the public welfare or, like George W. Bush, that the welfare of the oil industry is the public welfare. Ultimately, for all, domination is the name of the game, and in dominating one can produce some degree of integration and order.

---

* It has been said that if private enterprise cannot properly provide a managed health care, then the state must provide it. But these are not the only alternatives. Individuals can organise their own co-operative health service independent of state or capital.

Deceptive tricks are important techniques by which the state is enabled to maintain control with a minimum of effort. In its attempt to draw the allegiance of its subjects, the state will try to make it appear that it is a family or larger kinship group to which all belong. Kinship terms are frequently applied to rulers: the king is the father or grandfather, the queen is the mother and fellow citizens are brethren. The state also assumes the traditional functions of the family and clan. In modern times it has taken over the education of the young, the welfare of the needy, the protection of the homestead; it determines the limits to disciplining family members and attempts to manage life in the bedroom. Once, not long ago, the elderly and retired were supported by their kin group; now they depend upon old age pensions from the government. Increasingly the state has encroached upon and usurped the traditional role of the family and clan. In so doing it promotes a dependence upon the state. Indeed, the old dependence upon the family and other kin groups is transferred to the state. But the state is no loving mother. The more astute heads of state have calculated that it is cheaper in the long run to give the appearance of concern and direct some of the wealth to the common people and avoid otherwise discomforting altercations and revolts.

In many Asian and African states today the kinship network remains a determined competitor to the state. It challenges the state's claim to a monopoly of the use of violence by carrying on blood feuds; those who break the clan's code of honour are killed. But all states are having increasing access to highly sophisticated surveillance devices, transportation and armaments and so seek to suppress such activities. They may, however, be able to employ the kin group as a proper instrument of the state. The state arises when the kin groups yield to it.

## Trading

Practically any society engages in some sort of trading activity. It is part of the life of hunting-gathering peoples, whether Inuit in the far North or Australian Aboriginals and Bushmen in the South. And it may be even more important to horticultural and agricultural folk. In earlier societies trading was limited almost exclusively to luxury items. The necessities of life were all locally provided and only materials which were unavailable in the homeland were sought after. Even in Medieval times trade was limited to such things as spices, furs, precious metals, silk, quality horses and the like. Only modern states have come to trade in every conceivable item, and this may reach what appear to be ridiculous degrees, as when Canada exports lumber, pigs and cattle to the United States and the United States exports lumber, pigs and cattle to Canada.

Trading does not occur purely for the purpose of acquiring some goods. It is also an opportunity for making marital arrangements, for establishing diplomatic ties, for mutual planning for war against another group or for consolidating peace. Above all, it is a time for the exchange of ideas. New tools, techniques, medicines, religions, and a host of other practices and ideas, are spread in the trading context. The merchant trader has been a major vehicle for the spread of Islam into the African interior.

Trading entails points of trade – locations where goods are traditionally brought for exchange. These may be redistribution centres under the control of a Big Man, so that as chief trader he is able to enhance his wealth and power. They may also be market centres which eventually come to replace the redistribution system. Trading activity in such situations provokes a mixing of different peoples. To simplify relations a lingua franca is introduced as is a common 'currency' of some kind. The increasing complexity of trading activity and the greater the value of what is traded promote increasing hierarchical differences. Some individuals are already advantaged and in the competition of trade are able to garner to themselves further advantage so as to become bigger men standing at the threshold of state creation.

In Chapter 2 mention has already been made of stateless societies on the borders of giant states themselves engendering a state as a consequence of their proximity to those states and their trading activity with them.

For hundreds of years Badawin, among other desert nomads, operated a lucrative protection racket controlling trade routes and centres in the Sahara. This created a rather odd quasi-state condition in which the Badawin extracted tribute by force from the caravans and towns, leaving them otherwise to conduct their own affairs. The Badawin themselves maintained a political organisation in which the Big Men – the shaykhs – were first among equals unable to command as monarchs and forced to achieve their ends by influence, manipulation, cajoling and oratory.

In sum, trading is an important mechanism for expanding power and wealth and a major ingredient for state development.

## Specialised division of labour

In the section on kinship I have already touched on the significance of the division of labour to our topic. A division of labour based upon age and sex is a universal to all human societies: the specialised division is superimposed upon it, adding complexity and heterogeneity to a society. As has been noted, this makes for differences in interest and outlook and, hence, potential conflict. But, as Durkheim pointed out, it also makes for mutual interdependence – organic solidarity. Where only an age-sex division of labour occurs, as in a hunting-gathering society, each person is more a jack of all trades, although even here the mutual interdependence should not be overlooked for elders cannot do all the work of juniors and women are dependent upon men, just as men are dependent upon the women.

A specialised division of labour creates a hierarchy of crafts and professions. Some carry considerable prestige and power while others are inferior; some are despicable. The so-called caste system in India gave priority to a rigid ranking of occupations according to their ritual purity. The priests were at the top while cleaners of latrines, streets and such were 'untouchable'. It was a system based upon the ideology of inequality and one which clearly placed power in the hands of the most prestigious occupational groups.

Ancient Egypt did not have a caste system, but like that system, it made occupations largely hereditary and elevated priests, warriors and scribes to highest status. Similar arrangements were to be found in the other early states and much evidence indicates that there was a differentiation into superior and inferior type occupations prior to the full blossoming of any state. Powerful religious specialists and warriors were already clearly established, as were landowners and smiths, all of whom added to the bubbling stew which was to become the state.

## Property and the control of resources

The focus of the concept of property is on prior rights to exploit some thing; it is not on the thing directly. If a piece of land or an automobile is the property of Wycliffe, this means Wycliffe may use the property as he pleases within the limits set by law, while Tom, Dick and Harry may not use it without Wycliffe's permission. Wycliffe may drive his car only on any legal road; he may paint it green with black dots; he may even give it no oil so that the engine burns out. But he cannot drive it down the wrong side of the street or use it to run down pedestrians or smash other vehicles.

The idea of property reaches far back into antiquity. There does not appear to have been any primitive communism as dreamed by Marxists, although some very basic items may have been thought of as the property of a group, such as land and water. In a hunting-gathering society the territory within which it moves in search of food might be seen as the collective property of the local band. Tools, animals, houses were all individually owned; even among some there was private property of songs or fishing sites.

The farming lands associated with a village as a collective property of individuals who have kinship relations with the villagers may still be found in parts of Africa and Asia. Usually in this situation the village elders divide the arable land amongst the adult males, assigning equal plots to all. Within a fixed number of years all the plots are reassigned to different users. In this way over time each farmer will presumably have access to both the best and the poorest land. But this system is breaking down in favour of individual private property and in most of the world where there is agricultural activity farms are privately owned, leading to wild differences in the size of the holdings.

That some become large landlords and others very small ones or persons driven into landlessness results from a competition in which all do not start out on an equal playing field. It has not been uncommon for individuals to lose their property by the use of overt force by another. Some own land which is less productive; others are less astute and crafty in their business dealings, as others are superior con men. Many a person has lost the homestead through indebtedness and such indebtedness did not arise through laziness or drunkenness as so many conservatives would have it. A few do lose out because of their personal inadequacies. Some landholders are able to ingratiate themselves, or otherwise find favour with those having greater wealth and power, and extend their holdings. After all, one of the features of the Big Man is the ability to extend largess to his friends and flunkies, thus reinforcing the ties and securing their future support.

In the above discussion I have concentrated upon land because this is the most valuable resource in any agrarian society. Property in other resources has also been important. European colonialism instilled in many peoples new conceptions of property. The North American fur trade taught countless Indians that their trap lines were valuable assets to be protected from outside intruders. Amongst pastoralists livestock is individual property with which one can amass a fortune or descend into abject poverty. Pure luck may determine whether one man is wiped out by epidemic disease while another is able to keep a healthy herd. One loses stock to rustlers, while another is unharmed – he may even be the rustler. Land holdings with copper, gold or timber reserves afford yet further devices for acquiring wealth and power. Clearly property is a most important road to power, possibly the most important road. It is crucial for the elaboration of a redistribution system. Marxist theory identifies property accumulation with the evolution of the state, but since a most central part of the theory concerns class conflict I will reserve discussion of it for the following section on hierarchy.

## Hierarchic social order

Redistribution, the division of labour, trading and private property all produce social difference of a more fixed sort. Yet social differences are features of all societies. Australian Aboriginal society granted higher status to the elders of the band; women were inferior to men. A good hunter gained higher repute. Granted this is a simple kind of differentiation, but, it lays the basis for more elaborate forms. The differences amongst Australians or most any hunter-gatherer people were considered so minimal that such societies were called egalitarian and compared to most other societies they appeared so.

Rank societies, according to Fried, are those "in which positions of valued status are somehow limited so that not all those of sufficient talent to occupy such statuses actually achieve them. Such a society may or may not be stratified. That is, a society may sharply limit positions of prestige without affecting the access of its entire membership to the basic resources upon which life depends" (10). In a classification based on different criteria, Elman Service describes 'chiefdoms' as a type of society with close parallels to Fried's rank societies. "Chiefdoms are *redistributional societies* with a permanent central agency of co-ordination". The central agency acquires an economic, religious and political role (144). The redistributor of communal wealth is a person in an established position of influence, responsibility and wealth.

The political role of this redistributor varies considerably. At one pole we have the examples of the Yurok and Northwest Coast Indians who were subjected to diffuse and religious sanctions; their Big Men lacked authority to impose regulations. At the other extreme were some African and Polynesian redistributors who were petty kings, some with great authority. The important place of redistribution has already been discussed in an earlier section. But it is important to bear in mind that it is primarily through the evolution of a redistribution system that a ranking system becomes established. The redistribution may begin as a feast and the guests eventually become clients or dependents of the host, obligated to him as a feast sponsor. These obligations are reciprocated by the provision of goods and services to the feasting enterprise, which then becomes larger and more elaborate. The Big Men invent titles for themselves, assume a central role as mediators of disputes, assert supernatural claims, and as a result of their influence and growing status become central figures in trading activities. They are the holders of rank in the community. The redistribution system shifts from elaborate feasting in which there was once an equal distribution of goods to one favouring those with rank. Now the society may be said to be at the threshold of a stratified state, that is, provided the other factors we have discussed above, along with ideology, have also moved to favour greater stratification as well.

For Fried a "stratified society is one in which members of the same sex and equivalent age status do not have equal access to the basic resources that sustain life" (186). Here, resources is a term which is relative to a particular cultural context. Thus, for the Northwest Coast Indians of North America fish are a basic resource, but for the Indians of the Plains they were of no interest even though there were quantities in the rivers where they lived.

Stratified societies are invariably state societies. Fried, however, believed that there were stratified societies which lacked the state, although he says he could not find an example. I believe that there is one case of a stateless stratified society and that is ancient Iceland, although even this case is certainly arguable. Early Iceland, from the ninth to the eleventh centuries, was divided between freemen, who were the land-owners, and tenants and hired hands. From the freemen were drawn chiefs who, with their families, constituted a modest aristocracy. Like a Big Man a chief was involved in the redistribution of wealth and held periodic feasts. He enhanced his wealth by collecting fees and taxes and using his position to acquire land. Each chief was the senior man in his area, which included about a thousand inhabitants. He was the main decision maker to whom people deferred; he mediated disputes and sometimes attempted to punish culprits. While there was a vague legal sanction associated with the chief, he was primarily a man of influence who was successful in imposing his will to the extent that he could convince his followers to accept him as their first among equals. When the community withdrew its goodwill the chief was powerless. He had no police force to support him. The bad chief found his will frustrated, his following declining and ultimately his own demise. Individual freemen who disliked their chief might renounce their allegiance to him and accept another. The chiefdom was not a sovereign state, but was rather a voluntary contractual relationship between chief and freeman which could be broken at will by the freeman.

Beyond the local chiefdom, the only form of political integration in early Iceland centred around the 'Things'. These were voluntary judiciary assemblies of freemen led by the chiefs "where mutual problems were discussed according to orderly traditional procedures" (Thompson, 165). There were regional Things and one Althing for the whole island. None of the Things were truly governmental institutions since they had no power to enlist a police force nor any other means to enforce their decisions other than by diffuse sanctions which included banishment and confiscation of property. These were diffuse sanctions because enforcement depended upon the willingness of the populace to enforce the punishment, which usually meant that it was the aggrieved who might try to deal with the problem. Often judgments went un-enforced while any attempt to confiscate property ended in feuds.

One of the main reasons this kind of decentralised polity lasted as long as it did was that the several chiefs were jealous of their realms of power and so attempted to discourage any centralisation of authority. However, the struggle between chiefs eventually led to the supremacy of one chief who made Iceland a Norwegian dependency. Apparently a stratified stateless society would be a highly unstable entity, as it would also be a most improbable one, and, as the Icelandic example shows, it would bear too many state-like features.

Therefore, I believe stratified societies with only the rarest exceptions would have a state structure. This would be only reasonable and predictable. Once one has an aristocracy all the trappings of government are going to be established by that stratum in order to protect its position and interests. An aristocracy would already have an adequate infrastructure and sufficient resources well in place so that the creation of a state would be like placing the capping stone on a structure. As was noted above, a rank society may reach a position in which it is transformed into a stratified one. At the same time there have been countless egalitarian societies which have been catapulted into the state by being gobbled up by some colonial power.

These facts raise the issue of whether there are fixed stages through which all societies must pass in their evolution. In his *Ancient Society* Lewis Henry Morgan presented an elaborate scheme of seven stages through which societies presumably pass. There were three stages of savagery: lower, middle and upper – and three similar stages of barbarism, all culminating in civilisation. Each stage had numerous distinct characteristics, so that presumably one could review all contemporary or past societies and place them in one stage or another. Thus, lower savagery was made up of the simplest stone tool-using hunter-gatherers. It was the most backward, most 'primitive' stage of human existence. The highest achievements of humankind were to be found at the highest level of development, that of civilisation. True civilisation entailed metallurgy, writing, cities, agriculture, monotheism and the state. As others have pointed out before, the description of civilisation fitted quite well the New York state culture of Lewis Henry Morgan's home. And this suggests the highly ethnocentric nature of such a classification. Another problem is that it equates evolution with progress. Evolution is divergence of forms with common descent; there is no judgment as to whether it is good, bad, progressive or not. Progress is a value judgment; one measures progress against some desirable goal.

A third and most important difficulty with this theory of unilineal evolution is that it hardly fits the empirical data. Characteristics allegedly integral to one stage of development are found amongst people who, in every other respect, should be classed in another.

No one will deny that all human societies until ten thousand or so years ago were roughly of the 'savage' type, nor will they deny that the historical development of a large number of societies, especially those with which Europeans have been most familiar, have passed, very roughly, through these several stages. The tiny handful of pristine states also share a parallel evolution that would apply. But as some blanket scheme applicable to all societies it simply does not work.

Defenders of unilineal evolution have argued that there are two kinds of evolution: specific and general. The first applies to the study of specific cultures, an approach which, as I have said, does not work. General evolution looks at culture as a single phenomenon – culture in 'general'. There are two major problems with this. First, how does one derive the general from the specific? Every attempt is clearly distorted by a Eurocentric vision. Secondly, if one wishes to speak of a culture in general he has a case of one, a unique case, which makes scientific analysis impossible, since one cannot make a generalisation from one example alone.

Julian Steward thought cultural evolution concerned observable regularities in the process of cultural change and the task of the evolutionist is the empirical demonstration of what these regularities are. He argued for a multilineal evolution in which one might map out different sequences of the evolutionary process. This would seem to be a more productive approach and especially applicable to the evolution of the state.

Other evolutionary schemes have also been suggested, largely modelled on Morgan's unilinear evolution. Marx combines evolution with dialectic and conflict theory to produce an analysis of social class and state development. Marx accepts Morgan's evolutionary sequence, but he is primarily interested in changes which have occurred within civilisations and since the appearance of individual property. The earliest stages of human evolution were conceived as a time of primitive communism which, as has already been noted, is at best an overstatement of the actual situation. For Marx it is with the appearance of individual private property during 'barbarian' times that we have the commencement of a movement towards the state. For property accumulation means the rise of a propertied class which in turn exploits the non-propertied and makes them ever more dependent and depressed. In order to protect their interests the propertied create a state and it has served the wealthy throughout history, whether these were large landowners or, in modern times, capitalists. Competing economic classes produce conflict within the society eventually resulting in an open clash of interests. The English Revolution of mid-seventeenth century was a conflict between an old land-owning class and a rising bourgeoisie which eventuated in the triumph of capitalism. This conflict in turn has generated yet another dialectic process pitting capitalists against proletariat which it is believed will eventually produce a new synthesis in communism.*

The Marxists Barry Hindess and Paul Hirst have claimed that with "the primitive and advanced communist modes of production" there is no state because there are no social classes. Such a view ignores the bureaucratic managerial elite as a social class, thus unveiling one of the weaknesses of Marxist analysis. That is, the bureaucrats as non-property holders are not seen as a class and so are unworthy of further consideration. Yet they are, nevertheless, a potent social force which perpetuates the division

---

* The dialectic is no universal social process. First, there is no reason to believe that every cultural system must resolve its conflicts. Cultures may well persist by riding on their internal conflicts and achieving a kind of dynamic equilibrium through the balanced opposition of the conflicting forces. Even granting eventual resolution of a conflict does not mean it will be a synthesis. The dialectic allows for a variety of explanations because it is so ambiguous. It seems perfectly legitimate to argue that capitalism as an ideology is one thesis which generates an opposing thesis of socialism and the synthesis of the two is fascism (where capitalist private property is retained and socialist governmental control instituted). Finally, in the case of the Marxian dialectic, are we to assume that once communism has been achieved there will be no more conflict and so no need for a dialectic process?

of society into the powerful and powerless. Such observations are not intended to demonstrate the falsity of a class theory of state origin. Rather it is intended to question the absoluteness and dogmatism with which this theory is sometimes enunciated. Modern world events have demonstrated that a dominant ruling group or 'class' need not be the capitalists or anyone cornering the wealth of society. The technocratic-bureaucratic-military element prevails in much of the world and is fierce competition in the rest. Neither government nor social class (however it might be composed) can be developed to any extent without the other; they must develop in tandem.

A slight modification of Morgan's scheme was developed by Elman Service and Marshall Sahlins with special reference to the evolution of social organisation. In their view the elementary form of social organisation is the band which evolves into the tribe and it, in turn, transforms into a chieftaincy which can become a state. The band has actually the social characteristic of Morgan's savagery; the tribe and chieftaincy, his barbarism.

The band, which they claim is the characteristic of Paleolithic cultures, is a small (30-100 individuals), hunting gathering group of persons related by descent or marriage. At least in all bands there is a central core of related individuals. There is little quarrel with the notion of the band. It is with the remainder of their proposal that should be rejected.

It is said that the band evolves into a tribe – apparently that it must do so; it cannot jump directly to chieftaincy. The tribe is an association of kin segments or 'pan-tribal sodalities'. One type of tribe is that with a segmentary lineage like the Nuer, Tiv or any number of other Sub-Saharan peoples. Another is a cognitive group "composed simply of descendants traced through either or both mother's and father's relatives" (Service, 124). The cognitic pattern is found in Polynesia and among the Amhara of Ethiopia and in the Scottish clan system. Tribes also include the several peoples in Africa who have elaborate age classes and grades as well as others elsewhere who have warrior societies or men's clubs. The only possible significant feature of tribal societies which could be relevant to the evolution of the state is these men's groups. One hundred years ago Heinrich Schurtz proposed that they could well have been routes to the evolution of the state. They do provide an additional structure within the society and reinforce male dominance, but how, otherwise, do they contribute to the origin of the state? Men's societies as found in New Guinea are parts of social structures which have already achieved the status of simple rank type societies. Warrior societies such as existed among the Indians of the American Plains are parts of band organisations. Age grades and age classes are mostly in East Africa where they function alongside of segmentary lineages. They may give a temporary prestige and power to a segment of the elderly male population, but that is withdrawn after a few years as the incumbent elders retire and a new group assumes pre-eminence. There is no way any single person or group can manipulate the system so as to perpetuate a senior position, let alone establish a dynasty.

Presumably stages in an evolutionary sequence should be somehow preparatory for the stages to come. Here the ultimate goal of the process is the achievement of the state, so that the character of any tribal level or stage should be less egalitarian than the band and indicative of more social differences. But such is not the case. Among the cognitive groups mentioned above most of the Polynesians – such as Hawaiians and Tongans – and all of the Amhara and Scots are or were part and parcel of already existing states. For the remaining so-called tribal peoples the egalitarianism of the band is no less in the tribe. As in the band so in the tribe, differences arise out of age and sex. As in the band, so in the tribe, it is possible for individuals to rise in notoriety as a religious specialist or as a warrior. But there is nothing in the tribal situation, anymore than in the band, which really prefigures social stratification. The tribe does not appear to be a stage in the direct line of evolution to the state. Fried suggests the proper place for the tribe is as a dead end offshoot from the band ( 173).* It would be another evolutionary line.

The chiefdom has already been mentioned. Here I would only like to note that as a category it includes an enormous variety of quite different social organisations. In large part this difficulty arises from the fact that the definition of chiefdom centres on redistribution which itself is more of an umbrella term, an issue discussed in the section on Redistribution. The chiefdom category is made to include Northwest Coast hunter-gatherers carrying on potlatches, New Guinean Big Men sponsoring feasts, and the kings of simple states like ancient Hawaii or the many such entities in Sub-Saharan Africa. Obviously an enormous gulf separates the administration of the king of Bunyoro from the role of a Kwakiutl potlatch sponsor. Be that as it may, redistribution is a major vehicle in pushing a society towards the state. Fried's sequence proceeding from egalitarian to rank and to stratified society derives in a much modified fashion from Morgan, but has fewer pitfalls since it focuses directly on the question of status and at the same time simplifies the sequence of changes. What I suggest is that any stratified society will have the characteristic features delineated in this chapter and it would, therefore, be a state. Further, any society characterised by an elaborate redistribution system in which wealth is siphoned off to a dominant power elite would be a stratified state society.

## Ideology

By ideology I include the Marxist interpretation, that is, a grand delusional set of beliefs imposed by the ruling class upon the

---

* There are, of course, many definitions of the tribe. Here I deal only with tribe as conceived by Service.

exploited masses. This definition, however, is entirely too narrow. An ideology is more broadly any set of beliefs, explicit or implicit, which acts as a guide for daily living and an explanation of the world. The point is that a society, especially one which is highly specialised and multicultural, may have several, often competing, ideologies. The most popular one is that associated with the dominant group and it will be the one which is preached in its schools, most of its religious edifices and elsewhere.

In materialist theory, which seems so popular today, ideology is a pure epiphenomenon of the basic economic-technological aspects of society; it is a by-product which allows of no causal significance itself. Max Weber, among others, well demonstrated that ideology was indeed a potent force in all social affairs and one to be reckoned with in its own right. Thus, he showed that capitalism was not purely the natural result of ongoing economic processes, but was assisted in its flowering by the presence of a way of thinking, an outlook on life, that he called the Protestant ethic, and is now more commonly referred to by the more secular term, the work ethic.

Mao tse Tung, although a Marxist, observed that the economic forces alone were not transforming China into the communist wonderland. He, therefore, made every effort to instill in the Chinese a will to achieve that end. An ideology of work and devotion to the charismatic leader and the state was imperative for success.

No doubt a good majority of Americans* accept a common ideology which has been foisted on them since their kindergarten years. It goes something like this: America (sic) is the greatest

---

* For the citizens of the United States of America to call themselves Americans seems a little arrogant. After all, the great majority of people who live in 'America' (North and South America) are not citizens of the United States. Aren't they still Americans? Canadians sometimes refer to themselves as North Americans and kindly include the people of the US, but not the Mexicans or any other Central Americans who all also live in North America.

country in the world. It seeks only what is right and good; it has never engaged in an aggressive or unjust war; it is a land where freedom reigns and there is opportunity for anyone with spunk and ambition to become a 'success'. The only correct way to make decisions is through majority vote.* And the only proper economy is 'free enterprise'. And so on it goes.

Ideologies may be a congeries of sometimes conflicting or unrelated notions and there is usually a gulf between what is stated as ideal and what is reality or the existent fact. There is, of course, a fundamental problem in attempting to discern the ideology associated with the thousands of archaic cultures in the world. The archaeological record consists of material remains (this is why so many archaeologists are materialists). At best, one might make broad speculations about ideology from such data, but on the whole this are not helpful. On rare occasions there are written records. Yet the earliest of these provide little inkling as to ideology, being merely names of kings or bookkeeping accounts. On occasion there appear such gems as this from ancient Egypt: "Bow thy back to thy superior, thy overseer from the palace. (Then) thy household will be firmly fixed in its property, and thy reward will be as it should be. Opposition to a superior is a difficulty, because one lives as long as he is mild." Or another, also from Egypt: "If thou art one of those sitting at the table of one greater than thyself, take (only) what he may give, when it is set before thy nose. Thou shouldst gaze at what is before thee; do not pierce him with many stares, (for such) an aggression against him is an abomination to the *ka*. Let thy face be cast down until he addresses thee, and thou shouldst speak (only) when he addresses thee. Laugh after he laughs, and it will be pleasing to his heart and what thou mayest do will be pleasing to the heart" (from Wilson, 94).

---

* Some naive American Roman Catholics don't see why their church cannot be run by majority vote. But the Pope is not amused.

Essential to the existence of any state is an ideology of superiority/inferiority, of ruler and ruled; that it is only right and proper that persons holding certain offices should be above others and enjoy the legitimate right to compel others to obey them. In societies characterised by the presence of ranks this kind of ideology is not fully developed. There may be a recognition that some individuals are better or superior, but not sufficiently so to be a ruler commanding obedience. The appearance of a stratified elite system provides for a ruler, sustained by the kind of ideology expressed by the Egyptians above.

One of the reasons Christianity and Islam have been so successful is because their monotheism appeals to the rulers of states, since the notion of one god reinforces that of a single supreme ruler.

Almost all ideologies are founded in religious belief if they are not complete religious systems themselves. Such beliefs are expressed and reaffirmed by ritual practices. A.M. Hocart stressed the role of ritual in state formation. He wrote: "This ritual organisation is vastly older than government, for it exists where there is no government and where none is needed. When, however, society increases so much in complexity that a coordinating agency, a kind of nervous system, is required, that ritual organisation will gradually take over this task." He goes on to say that to "our intellectuals only economic interests can create anything as solid as the state. Yet if they would only look about them they would everywhere see communities banded together by interest in a common ritual; they would even find that ritual enthusiasm builds more solidly than economic ambitions because ritual involves a rule of life, whereas economics are a rule of gain, and so divide rather than unite" (35).

The history of early states clearly demonstrates the immense importance of religious ideology. Pharaoh was a god-king and the temple, the priests, the ritual and myth were integral to the maintenance of the entire state apparatus. Similarly in Sumer, and later Babylon, the temple and the priest provided the ideology identifying the state with divinity. Throughout history little has changed. Even in the United States, presumably a secular state which keeps the church allegedly divorced from the state, religious ideology is invoked to provide the underpinning for the whole structure. God is continually called upon in the halls of Congress; god and mammon are made one in the currency; god and nation are made one in a pledge of allegiance.

While the old Soviet Union and its Communist satellites did not invoke the name of god, they all gave a strong religious ritual bent to their so-called communism. Marx and Engels works were treated like Bibles; their enormous portraits like holy icons; their persons like prophets; there were hymns and grand processions. They did not have god, but they had the dialectic.

Everywhere it appears the state must justify itself by reliance upon some extra-human, superhuman power. The ideology gives legitimacy to the state.

Before concluding this chapter it is necessary to explain why writing has not been included in the list of essentials for state development. It is indeed difficult to imagine how a state could survive for long without some techniques for recording necessary information. And so it is true that the great majority of states did have access to a writing system, but there are enough which did not to justify excluding it from the list. The Peruvian states, the majority of those in pre-colonial Sub-Saharan Africa, and those in ancient Polynesia all lacked writing.

## Conclusion

The state is an emergent out of the interacting preparatory factors discussed in this chapter. Using another metaphor one may say that all these factors converge in slightly different ways so that a given society slides down a slippery slope to the state condition.

There is a mutilineal evolution wherein in one case there is an intensive elaboration of the redistribution system or, in another, more emphasis on the military and so on; there are different emphases and different styles and impetuses. Population, sedentarism, agriculture, a complex division of labour, a redistribution system and private property constitute a kind of platform upon which hierarchy and an ideology of superiority/inferiority are built. It might be possible that a society with only a weakly developed hierarchic social order and ideology of superiority/inferiority could avoid the descent into statehood. This is even more likely where private property is not of major importance. Examples of such a phenomenon are most likely to be found in the acephalous societies of pre-colonial Africa. The moment of state creation occurs when all the factors, however achieved, fall into place. This is so for pristine and secondary states. The latter, despite having the state imposed upon them, would still have had to develop those preparatory characteristics in some minimal fashion in order to maintain a state.

No state would ever develop if there were no drive on the part of at least some individuals to acquire power over others and at the same time a conditioning of a great majority of the populace to submit to the power of the few. We must acknowledge that entrenched in the human psyche is a potentiality for a will to power as there is at the same time a potentiality for a will to submit and a will to freedom. Once there is a state apparatus it becomes important for those in power to devote considerable resources to inculcating a submissive mentality, a child-like dependency.

It is a very common argument that there must be a central organisation and control in a society or all will be bloodshed. Acephalous, anarchic social organisation is widespread. It should also be emphasised that acephaly or self-organisation is a major principle for ordering the universe. Unless one hypothesises some kind of god (a hypothesis which is impossible to substantiate) one must conclude that the ordering of the elements, of the galaxies, and the solar system, of life forms themselves are all the products of self-organising mechanisms. There is no Central Committee, no president who ordered life to develop as it has. Such development is the consequence of the interaction and interbreeding of countless individuals who had and have no idea of what in fact results. Life forms are emergents out of the acts of individual organisms operating with a few basic principles.

In human societies the significance of self-organisation is primary and fundamental. Adam Smith wrote of the operation of the invisible hand. As he pointed out the division of labour emerged out of the activities of numerous inidviduals who were reacting to specific circumstances by each specialising in a given endeavour. Out of each separate activity there arose the complex system of the modern division of labour. The capitalist economy operates without central direction, but as a consequence of the interaction of various forces manipulated by individual humans.

We may say the same about language or culture as a whole. How did the English language originate and appear as it is today? More than a millenium ago several hundred thousand people interacting with each other, each drawing on his own personal experience and contacts with a variety of different factors, each employing a common antecedent language, engaged in a process which eventuated in modern English, a process unplanned, unconscious, uncontrolled by any central director. The culture of any given group or indeed, culture in general, is an emergent from the activity and interactivity of individuals who had no idea of what was resulting at the time.

It is sometimes remarked that the human body is ordered by its central control mechanism, the brain. But the brain itself is an immensely complex organ which must catalogue a great deal of information and deal with innumerable messages. And it has no central administration.

Everywhere order is created out of 'chaos' or a congeries by self-organising processes. Put another way, individuals (whether people, organisms, atoms or what) interact with the environment and produce as a consequence unintended and ordered results.

The notion that all phenomena require a head or must be controlled by a central organisation is a subterfuge promoted by the state. It is similar to another which holds that if there were no police and no jails all life would become utter chaos. Neighbour would commence butchering neighbour, husbands their wives, and everyone would break into stores to take whatever they pleased. But if humans were truly so inclined they would require a policeman for every person plus policemen to police the police, which is far from the reality. Few people are actually any threat to the public peace. There have been periods of natural disasters or such events as major power outages in large cities. In these situations there is some looting, but it is the work of a small minority, always the poor, the alienated and resentful, that is, those looking to some way to even the score with an exploitative, oppressive elite. The great majority of the population engage rather in mutual aid seeking to help the less fortunate. The police do exist as a show of force and are always ready and willing to demonstrate their capability, but the point is that the great majority of people have been adequately trained to respect certain rules to which they adhere whether or not the police are present. Therefore, while the state holds the club of force and violence over all our heads it relies more upon a proper training and conditioning of the citizenry to abide by the rules. This training commences at birth where the state relies upon the family to inculcate the young with all manner of regulations, but, especially, with a submission to authority (as conceived by the state). A Jesuit is alleged to have said that if you give him your child before age seven he will make a loyal and faithful member of the church. And so it is that the state will add its clout to that of the parents before the child is seven by providing for public schooling. Now the young are continually exposed to various rituals emphasising obedience and submission to the state: singing the national anthem (usually soaked in the blood of 'patriots'), raising the flag, saluting it and treating it with veneration. So-called history or social studies courses teach correct citizenship, glorify the state and justify its every act. In the upper grades there is often military training which only reinforces the idea of unquestioned obedience and the infallible nature of the state.

In addition to the family and the public schools a further 'educational' element is the religious institutions. It is not unusual that the religions which are most eager to impose submissiveness and deference to authority are precisely those which have been so successful – Christianity (especially in its Roman Catholic form) and Islam. In both cases they are obviously seen by the forces in control of the state as bulwarks to their efforts. For example, the aim of almost all Christian sects is to produce meek, quiet, unprepossessing souls more concerned with a supposed after-life than with this life. Even though a religion may commence as a competitor or opponent of the state, as was the probable case with Christianity, especially once it is able to convert a large proportion of the population, it is commandeered by the state, with the most common consequence being a marriage of church and state.

De la Boetie wrote that one reason people submit to the state is because they are born serfs and are reared as such. One may question the first part of this comment, but the more than five thousand year history of the state demonstrates we are reared to be serfs.

In addition to these forces inculcating submissiveness, de la Boetie argued that the state tricks us all into servitude. There are bread and circuses. Holidays are provided to glorify the state with plenty of flags, martial music, parades and patriotic speeches. The state provides welfare to the poor, pensions to the elderly and disabled, public thoroughfares, fire protection, education of the young and any number of other services. Thus it tricks the populace into greater and greater dependency and the belief that the state is indispensable. Of course, like any good farmer who wants to keep his livestock healthy, so the state, too, for its own well-being should be concerned with a healthy citizenry. But the best payoff of this approach is to reinforce popular devotion to the state and the belief that all remain helpless without the state.

Now it is perfectly true that even in a stateless society there is strong dependence upon the local group, a dependence upon magic and fear of diffuse sanctions such as gossip or personal injury.* Humans are social animals and none can go it completely alone. Nietzsche's idea of the Ubermensch (the overmen) may have a certain appeal in its aristocratic individualism, but it is unlikely that anyone could be so utterly self-reliant. Even Thoreau could not achieve independence. What is at issue here is that the state seeks to destroy any independent spirit. It makes us believe we could not have good roads unless the state provided them. It encourages the fear of freedom itself. Erich Fromm, in analysing Western European culture, argued that there is an escape from freedom. He deals with the Reformation pointing out that it freed men and women from the authority of the Roman Church, but this left everyone free to achieve salvation on his own and all by himself, a rather terrifying thought. Thus, one seeks to escape. One can find salvation in the all-embracing arms of a powerful state. This argument, of course, questions the extent to which humans can be free and that is a most valid and significant question. My point is that the state strives to make one fear freedom and question one's own capabilities.

One important trick of every well ordered state is the

---

* In a more desirable kind of anarchist society, of course, diffuse sanctions would be constructive and ameliorative.

manufacture of external enemies and the fear of outside threat to the sacred homeland. Few things can better consolidate a populace and make them forget the more real problems of their lives. Over its history the United States has manufactured a continual string of 'evil empires'. (Soviet Union, China, Vietnam, Cuba, Iran, Libya, North Korea and Iraq). The people of the United States remained quite reluctant to enter the Second World War until Roosevelt and his cronies concocted the 'cowardly sneak attack' on the sacred soil of America by the Japanese. Bush, the Younger, like his father before him promoted war on 'terrorist' Iraq.

There remains one more facet of the issue of how the state manages to lull us all into obedience. It is no accident that writing was invented within a state and at about the same time that the state first emerged. One has to have records of state properties, of taxes and tributes, of resources and of the whereabouts of the citizenry. The notion of the census is very ancient. From being a very simple operation of merely counting noses, it has ballooned like a giant cancer into the collection of a multitude of very personal data from each person. The state gains access to one's complete biography including who or what his/her sexual preferences might be. Failure to respond will land you in prison. Any information lacking from the census report can be acquired through one's tax report. For example, the Canadian government knows exactly how much money I earn; with the aid of the census material they could calculate my total worth and know all the sources of my wealth and where I deposit any savings. From the receipts I am required to give them, they know every ailment my wife or I have had along with its treatment and the names of the physicians providing the treatment. From receipts from charities and answers to questions on the tax form they can suspect my political, philosophical, religious and intellectual proclivities. The state seeks to delve into the deepest recesses of everyone's mind, the better to control. Modern surveillance devices add to this capability. There are a multitude of listening and seeing devices which make privacy a major luxury and such devices are not only available to the state, but to others as well, including the corporate world.

Every society has its share of so-called deviants, rebels and non-conformists. In part this is a result of less effective indoctrination, but also of the fact that people can only stand so much abuse. Revolts against the state have occurred throughout history and in probably every state. Peasant revolts characterise the five thousand year history of Egypt. And even the conservative and colourless Canadians have had their revolts. But revolts do not aim at any fundamental change in the system; they seek reforms, often quite petty reforms. Even revolutions which aim at more fundamental changes and complete removal of an existing ruling elite are rare and in the end accomplish little (e.g. the English, French, American, Russian and Chinese revolutions).

Lysander Spooner wrote that revolts are not that common because although people may see the evil of government they do not know how to get rid of it or do not wish to gamble their personal interests in attempting to do so. And Michael Mann claims that the reason the masses do not revolt is that they "lack collective organisation to do otherwise, because they are embedded within collective and distributive power organisations controlled by others. They are organizationally outflanked" (7).

# Chapter 4

# The Modern State and its Future

This essay has suggested that the peoples of the world have been hoodwinked into embracing the state and questions were raised as to why this should be so and how it came about. I hope that these pages have at least thrown some light on such questions.

To address them requires an understanding of the nature of the state. To understand the nature of the state requires a knowledge of its history and dynamics. It has been noted that in the course of its history the state has revealed one enduring and outstanding characteristic – despotism – and at the same time it instills a sense of dependence on the part of the individual. Until a little more than two centuries ago, practically all states have been either oligarchies, theocracies or absolute monarchies. Today, however, there are a number of alleged democracies which some argue are not despotic. But I have attempted to demonstrate that such an argument is an illusion. Democracy is at best the dictatorship of a majority and in practice it is the dictatorship of a plurality which is then really a minority. Further, democracies continue the despotic features of other polities: the hierarchy of the rulers and the ruled and the wealthy and the poor, compulsory membership, the obligation to obey all laws under pain of death or incarceration, the suppression of secession or separatism, the inculcation of a nationalist spirit, a devotion to military might, and the encouragement of submissiveness and dependence. Defiance of the state whether democratic or not means punishment; respect for authority and love of the state means reward.

A major concern of this essay has been with how a state is created and what the ingredients are that put it together. It was argued that the state arose out of a rank type society through the interaction of eleven significant elements (population, sedentary settlement, horticulture/agriculture, redistribution, military organisation, the secondary significance of kinship, trading, specialised division of labour, individual property and control of resources, hierarchic social order, and an ideology of superiority/inferiority). The state appears as a pristine institution in only a few places. Elsewhere it was copied from the original type, invariably under duress, and particularly when these societies themselves shared similar preparatory elements. The movement from a rank type society to the state need not be an inevitable event, although it is a major historical trend. Once the state has been instituted it acts as an iron grip upon society, so that while we can verify cases of a state's movement towards greater decentralisation and freedom or, conversely, a movement to greater centralisation and authoritarianism, there are no cases of the state abolishing itself in favour of a return to a pristine anarchy. And this is to be expected. After all, those invested with such power are going to be very reluctant to surrender it. Power does corrupt. It is the Siren call endured by Odysseus. But as I remarked in chapter 1, what is, is not necessarily what ought to be.

Today the state faces formidable competition from enormous international corporations each of which wields a subtle power mightier than that of dozens of states combined and wealthier than them as well. Unlike a state these corporations do not require a military force because the state, especially the United States and the United Kingdom, is already there to provide any necessary force. But the corporations are more often able to use their wealth to see that their will is done without relying upon the armies of the state.

All of the major corporations and most states in the world have formed a World Trade Organisation which is a secret enclave aimed to advance their financial interests in every nook and cranny of the earth. These interests take priority over the mundane state interests such that environmental regulations established by one government may be judged as hindering the developmental interests of the corporate world and so overruled. Thus, that state is required to water down or repeal its regulation and if it does not comply it will find itself under an international trade boycott which in this day and age means economic doom. Such actions are, of course, a direct threat to the sovereignty of the erring state and would not be enforceable without the support of those states which follow the appropriate regulation. This demonstrates that sovereignty is and always has been a relative privilege. The most powerful states reign. The United States would never have to face such shameful ends, first, because practically all of its interests are those of the giant corporations which are American anyway and, secondly, if it were challenged it would reject any claims out of hand.

It may be ironic that in Canada an organisation which makes the loudest protests against this incursion on states 'rights', the Council of Canadians, is supported by so many socialists and other left-wingers – ironic because their opposition essentially amounts to a vehement assertion of nationalism, genuflecting before the maple leaf to the sentimental refrain of 'O Canada'. If nothing else this demonstrates the socialist naïveté about the nature of power.

In the opposition to the World Trade Organisation there sometimes appears to be a panic that the giant corporations are going to gobble up one's national state. Rather the corporations are more dependent on the several major nation states. At the very least the corporations will form alliances with select states, helping them to prosper and maintain a superiority at the expense of the others. The corporations need the state to insure the protection of property, military interventions where necessary, subsidies and favourable regulations aimed to discourage opposition. Further, there is no reason to believe that the corporations would always remain some united front, some monolithic monster. They, too, can engage in feuding, factional conspiracies and plots, engaging the separate nation states, so as to create new cold wars or even hot wars.

Another area where the modern state appears threatened is in the various attempts to establish unions of states. First, there was the League of Nations and when that failed the idea revived with the United Nations. Now we also have the European Union. There are those who dream of a day when all individual states will be fully consolidated as a single world state and they see the United Nations as the embryo of such an institution. As it presently exists, however, the constitution of the United Nations is a long way from being a unitary state and it only demonstrates once again that the notion of state sovereignty is all relative. From the beginning the UN has been controlled through a veto power by five dominant members – the United States, the Soviet Union (now Russia), China, Britain and France. With the conflict in Iraq the United States has been able to act on its own and defy the UN. And the strong opposition of France, Germany and Russia to the United States regarding this war reflects those nations fear of the dominance of the United States and concern for their own importance in the power game. Even a small bellicose nation like Israel has been able to defy the UN proclamations against it on dozens of occasions primarily because behind it is the power of the United States.

To give the figment of equal sovereignty the General Assembly of the UN provides each member state with one vote so that Tuvalu or St Kitts are in that way equal to the United States or India, but the ultimate and final veto still depends upon the five major power players. Further, in the General Assembly the lesser powers are always at the mercy of the big predators who operate protection rackets threatening to withhold all sorts of goods and services or impose boycotts on those who do not comply with their wishes. A most memorable example was the vote on the creation of the state of Israel in 1948 when the United States threatened the Philippines and most Latin American countries with adverse consequences if they did not favour Israel. At the approach of the Iraqi war in 2003 the United States engaged in the most scandalous attempts at arm twisting and bribery to create 'allies'.

While the UN has established and operated many commendable organisations such as those connected with health and welfare and, on occasion, facilitated mediation in disputes between nations, it is no united nations. It was created by the five major powers as an instrument for their own purposes. And since the close of the twentieth century it has been the primary instrument of the United States.

It is the height of absurdity to believe that a sovereign state, especially any of the great power houses, will voluntarily abdicate any 'authority' to some other organisation without first receiving some considerable advantage to itself. States are not constructed any more than any other institution to oversee their own extinction. In fact this is least so for the state, which, as has been noted, is an investment in power and its jealous maintenance.

One may counter with the proposition that the European Union is an example of a union of states; but this really is an economic alliance where no one's sovereignty is being challenged or, if there is any sacrifice of that nature, it is clearly repaid in economic advantage or at least presumed economic advantage. Further, this union seems to be dominated by France and Germany and they certainly would not tolerate any action by the Union which was not in their interests.

European Union, United Nations, League of Nations – all are devices for advancing the special political-economic interests of the advantaged and most predatory states and if they are not advanced through these bodies they are summarily ignored. If by a slim chance a true united nations should ever be created, it would be because a single state has achieved world hegemony and sees it to its advantage to allow for such an entity, which would only be its plaything. The United States today, as the only superpower, seems to be aspiring for this role.

Incidentally, a single world state would be a most bizarre and unique phenomenon. States have always thrived on competition and war with other states: what will now be the spirit stimulating the world state? There must be some 'evil empire' elsewhere,* lest the attention of the 'masses' be allowed to turn to their own disadvantaged condition. The enormous size and power in a government of a world state surely boggles the mind. So far at least, if one were so dissatisfied with the government of his homeland, he could flee to another place which was presumably less abusive. How could one flee from the world state? Could one of the motives for the space programs be the search for another 'evil empire', certainly not a search for a place of refuge?

There is no reason to believe that a multitude of states dominated by super powers will not persist into the future. However, what would lead to social collapse is a monumental nuclear or environmental disaster. By the latter I mean that with future population increases to the ten to twelve billion mark there will arise overwhelming pressures on land and resources. Soil, water and air will be increasingly polluted. Available potable water in vast areas of the earth will reach crisis proportions. Soils and energy and other resources could well become exhausted. The earth can readily become a desolate wasteland best suited for cockroaches. Thus far, states have not taken any potential environmental crisis seriously, arguing that profits are prior. However, should the situation become sufficiently acute state

---

* *Cf.* remarks by Von Treitschke in chapter III.

reactions, in a desperate attempt to stem the tide, would readily resort to increasingly authoritarian procedures, along with other practices which would hasten environmental catastrophe and chaos. In such an event it could be that those which have been least involved in the industrial-technological-developmental system will survive. Yet given the present rate of involvement – growth? – there may not be any such places left.

I am reminded of the Mad Max movies where the world has become a gigantic wasteland inhabited by rival gangs and in *Beyond Thunderdome* there is a quite degenerate town, Bartertown, which 'thrives' as a source of fuel manufactured from the methane derived from the wastes of a herd of pigs. The town is ruled by two competing individuals: one is Tina Turner, the queen, while the other is the Master, a dwarf who manages and controls the fuel production and rides around on the back of a powerful giant. The dwarf is able to maintain ultimate power until the giant is killed, thus leaving the tiny dwarf on the ground at risk of being trampled by all of the pigs. Some distance from Bartertown is an isolated refugee community of children. They are apparently a bit more human, more innocent and stable than the Bartertown crowd and are waiting for a saviour to take them 'home'.

These pessimistic views of the future are clearly more believable today. And, of course, even they offer some glimmer of hope, if that is what the community of children is supposed to be. Perhaps as a modification of this Mad Max tale, one could conceive of the possibility of building free alternative structures even in the midst of an increasing barbarism. This was the suggestion of Gustav Landauer who urged that we ignore the state as much as possible and proceed to create areas of freedom and mutualism. I would call them Permanent Autonomous Zones (PAZ) rather than the Temporary Autonomous Zones (TAZ) of Hakim Bey. Voluntary cooperative societies can be organised, each dealing with a specific problem: education, health, sale of consumer goods, fire protection and so on. While most attempts to form communes or utopian communities have failed, a few have survived and could serve as positive examples to the extent that they are liberatory. Above all, we can be more kind to the earth and support efforts for a cleaner land. In addition, we can seek to extend the realm of those diffuse sanctions which are non-violent and positive, and aim for conflict resolution rather than being punitive and destructive.

A number of worthwhile negative activities include minimising one's taxable income, not voting or serving on juries, rejecting military training and government employment and refusing to support or endorse unethical enterprises.

None of this may make much of a dent in the establishment, but these things must be done if only to retain our humanity. Even if we descend to a Mad Max world, it should be the believers in freedom and justice who comprise the enclaves of refugee children.

# BIBLIOGRAPHY

Assmann, Jan, *The Mind of Egypt* (Metropolitan Books, Henry Holy: New York, 2002)

Barclay, Harold B., *People without Government: An Anthropology of Anarchy* (Kahn and Averill: London, 1982 and 1990)

Barnard, Alan, *History and Theory in Anthropology* (Cambridge University Press, 2000)

Bey, Hakim, *Temporary Autonomous Zones* (Automedia: Brooklyn, 1991)

de la Boetie, Etienne, *The Politics of Obedience* (Free Life editions: New York, 1975)

Byock, Jesse, *Viking Age Iceland* (Penguin, 2001)

Carneiro, Robert, 'Political Expansion as an Expression of the Principle of Competitive Exclusion' in Cohen and Service

Clastres, Pierre, *Society Against the State* (Urizen: New York, 1977)

Cohen, Ronald, 'State Foundations: A Controlled Comparison' in Cohen and Service

Cohen, Ronald and Service, Elman (editors), *Origin of the State* (Institute for the Study of Human Issues: Philadelphia, 1978)

Dahrendorf, Ralf, *Class and Class Conflict in Industrial Society* (Stanford,1959)

Engels, Frederick, *The Origin of the Family, Private Property and the State* (Pathfinder: New York, 1972)

Firth, Raymond, *Essays on Social Anthropology and Values* (Athlone: London, 1964)

Fried, Morton, *The Evolution of Political Society* (Random House, 1967)

Fromm, Erich, *Escape from Freedom* (Avon: New York,1941)

—, *Man for Himself* (Rinehart,1947)

Gluckman, Max, *Politics, Law and Ritual in Tribal Society* (Aldine,1965)

Goodman, Paul, *Drawing the Line* (Random House, 1946)

Haas, Jonathan, *The Evolution of the Prehistoric State* (Columbia University Press,1982)

Hindess, Barry and Paul Hirst, *Pre-Capitalist Modes of Production* (Routledge & Kegan Paul, 1975)

Hocart, A. M., *Kings and Councillors* (Chicago, 1970)

Hoffman, Michael A., *Egypt before the Pharaohs* (University of Texas, 1991)

Ibn Khaldun, *The Muqaddimah* (Princeton, 1974)

Kraeling, C.H. and Adams, R.M. (editors), *City Invincible: An Oriental Institute Symposium* (Chicago, 1960)

Kroeber, Alfred, *Configurations of Culture Growth* (California, 1944)

Lehning, Arthur (editor), *Michael Bakunin: Selected Writings* (Grove Press: New York, 1973)

Lesko, Barbara, 'Rank, Roles and Rights' in *Pharaoh's Workers* edited by Leonard H. Lesko (Cornell, 1994)

Maine, Henry, *Ancient Law* (Murray: London, 1861)

Maisels, Charles Keith, *The Emergence of Civilization* (Routledge, 1993)

Malinowski, Bronislaw, *Crime and Custom in Savage Society* (Kegan Paul, Trench and Trubner, 1932)

Mann, Michael, *The Sources of Social Power, volume 1* (Cambridge, 1986)

Milgrim, Stanley, *Obedience to Authority* (Harper & Row, 1974)

Morgan, Lewis Henry, *Ancient Society* (J.C. Saha Roy: Calcutta, 1958)

Nadel, S. F., *Black Byzantium* (Oxford, 1942)

Oppenheimer, Franz, *The State* (Free Life Editions: New York, 1975)

Parsons, Talcott, 'The Distribution of Power in American Society' in *Structure and Process in Modern Societies* (Free Press: New York, 1960)

Proudhon, Pierre Joseph, *The General Idea of the Revolution in the Nineteenth Century* (Freedom Press: London, 1923)

Radcliffe-Brown, A.R., *Structure and Function in Primitive Society* (Free Press: Glencoe, Illinois, 1952)

Saggs, H.W. F., *The Greatness that was Babylon* (Mentor: New York, 1962)

Schneider, Harold K., *Livestock and Equality in East Africa* (Indiana University Press, 1979)

Service, Elman, *Primitive Social Organisation* (2nd Edition, Random House, 1971)

Skocpol, Theda, *States and Revoution* (Cambridge,1979)

Sahlins, Marshall and Service, Elman, *Evolution and Culture* (University of Michigan, 1960)

Southall, A. W., *Alur Society* (W. Heffer & Sons: London, 1954)

Steward, Julian H, *Theory of Culture Change* (University of Illinois, 1955)

Thompson, Laura, *The Secret of Culture* (Random House, 1969)

Turner, Victor, *The Ritual Process* (Aldine, 1969)

Tylor, Edward B., *Anthropology* (Watts: London, 1946)

Von Treitschke, H., *Politics* (Harcourt, Brace & World, 1963)

Weber, Max, *The Theory of Social and Economic Organisation* (Free Press, 1964)

Wheatley, Paul, *The Pivot of the Four Quarters* (Edinburgh University Press, 1971)

Wilson, John A., *The Culture of Ancient Egypt* (Chicago, 1951)

Wittfogel, Karl A., *Oriental Despotism* (Yale, 1963)